Future for Youth Employment:
New Changes in Approaches to Business
Book I

by Eva Kras and contributors

© Copyright 2018 Eva Kras and contributors

ISBN 978-1-63393-696-6

All rights reserved. No part of this publication may be reproduced, stored in a retrieval system, or transmitted in any form or by any means—electronic, mechanical, photocopy, recording, or any other—except for brief quotations in printed reviews, without the prior written permission of the author.

Review copy: this is an advanced printing, subject to corrections and revisions.

Published by

210 60th Street
Virginia Beach, VA 23451
800-435-4811
www.koehlerbooks.com

With Pleasure!
Eva Kras

FUTURE FOR YOUTH EMPLOYMENT

NEW CHANGES IN APPROACHES TO BUSINESS

BOOK ONE

EVA KRAS
& Contributors

VIRGINIA BEACH
CAPE CHARLES

PREFACE

Eva Kras

Our world is in turmoil. What will it be like in twenty to twenty-five years, when present-day toddlers graduate from high school and universities? These are issues that parents of young people are presently pondering. Every indication points to some large changes in how they will live.

This book is concerned primarily with the theoretical background necessary for future employment. It includes a group of papers by researchers—mainly senior university research, from Europe, North America, and Latin America. They each examine different aspects of future youth employment. For the reader, this translates to what we need to do over the next few years to have a favorable environment for the future of youth employment. The main area includes the study of the small business sector, small co-operatives, and some NGOs. This includes various subjects related to a "longer distant future," that is, twenty to twenty-five years hence.

Some key ideas include such subjects as beliefs and concerns of youth, the formation of solid communities (where these small businesses are and where owners live and work), and the problems of the country of living at large. We see these items as fundamentally different from the majority of business atmospheres today.

GENERAL AREAS TO CONSIDER FOR THE SMALL BUSINESS SECTOR

The Monied and Short-Term Society

Most of our youth have been or will be exposed to, in the shorter term, a society based on money as well as the dominance of the large business sector in most countries.

Twenty to twenty-five years hence, we will see this situation changing in society. Shortage of work will not be the huge problem it is today. Instead, the youth will have received a change in the educational system. Then they will see some business thinking and instruction in high school, postsecondary, and university education—all directed to the small business sector, not the large, usually international sector we have today.

Also, how students feel and think about their future employment will be different. They will most likely replace our monied and fast-moving society with smaller organizations in all their forms, such as SMEs, cooperatives, and some NGOs. A few large corporations will always continue to exist, as some countries need certain natural resources for even small companies, but they will not dominate as they have.

Such varied types of small business will satisfy young graduates' energy, imagination, and desire for a challenge. All of this development, however, depends heavily on the backing and comfort young people receive from strong local communities. These communities will welcome new small businesses which satisfy the needs for stimulation of youth, as well as trust and sharing (rather than present-day competition).

These communities also form the basis for local export (whether intranational or within close neighborhoods). The solidity of these communities is what allows the small business sector to flourish.

Modest Income

Those who run small businesses must also become satisfied with **modest income,** in place of looking for work "that provides the most money." The term "modest income" can have many different meanings, depending on where we live. The expression refers to people in general, as presently we are trying to base our societies on the "money society."

Therefore, we should say modest incomes should allow us to live decently, that is, have enough good food to eat, a simple but adequate home, schools for children, and medical coverage. Society, in general, should measure us not in monetary terms, but on personal merits, and our practice of habits we strongly value. It has been said many times that we are replacing a "monied society'" and how the world sees us with something more valuable and fulfilling to people. Youth will be able to find peace and happiness in daily life, even to "invent" them.

Governments

This whole new world of the small business sector will also mean many changes for governments, forcing them to think in the longer term in how they develop their nations and in how they plan and prioritize for funding. This is of course very different from today's thinking, but many researchers view it as a helpful shift from our present-day scenario of large businesses and lack of employment except for a few.

We must remember, this involves the future of youth employment, twenty to twenty-five years hence, and therefore, the papers which follow will treat different aspects given our future involvement.

These papers include the following areas for our future:

1.) How We Think: Present and Future.
2.) Economic
3.) Community Development
4.) Ecology
5.) Generational differences
6.) Education

We must also bear in mind that, to make major changes in our development and seriously consider the very young generation of children now, we need to begin "backcasting" to attain significant changes for our future.

As this small book is devoted to the future, let us first look at some indicators for human development and "social entrepreneurship" from well-known organizations like the Skoll Foundation. Based on indications made by the president and CEO of Skoll, Sally Osberg:

"Social entrepreneurs deeply understand that human dignity depends on the security that comes from knowing fundamental needs are met: health, food, shelter, and safety . . . Only when those needs are fulfilled can all people achieve their full potential."

This statement brings us to the future of employment of youth, and SMEs for many stable and lifelong communities. This presumes a difficult struggle between our present day "money-based society" and making "humanity" a priority in society in general. The following involves a few examples of what we mean by SMEs and the priority placed on humanity in the future.

HUMANITY AND THE FUTURE OF SMES

1.) This outline involves jobs for youth in SMEs for the future in three areas: Europe, North America, and Latin America.
2.) These jobs are based on the importance of SMEs and strong communities.
3.) Strong communities are essential for the development of strong SMEs, who employ many youths and rely on their deep imaginations.
4.) Sharing of knowledge is important and must be prioritized above "go it alone" and the concept of competition. Instead, youth will look at "togetherness" as a form of strength.
5.) Modest but decent income in place of "money" should be the first consideration. In the ideal system, people come to value a new type of respect which does not include money as such.

6.) SMEs expand feelings of innovation and personal satisfaction at work.
7.) Youths begin to see "the needs" of an established community as important. They begin to trust each other and talk to each other differently as they begin to see the opportunities for SMEs.
8.) Youths tend to see long-term considerations for families and all generations.
9.) This new source of employment for youths also requires new forms of thinking and new styles of "education for smaller business."

These points refer to the theoretical basis for stable, lifelong employment for youth. Surprising examples of this way of thinking and working already exist on different continents. The next book will include examples of small companies that already exist.

The following papers, as outlined below cover many subjects related to SMEs in the future. The variations are significant, and the magnitude of change is great. Each of these papers looks at new ideas for employment of youth for the future. We hope those ideas inform the thinking of our readers.

This book will not provide a specific method of how these changes will work, as each country is different, even though many of the basic ideas are in common in Europe, North America, and Latin America, the areas on which we based this study.

We are hoping that the readers will find, on the whole, a new era of thinking is possible for the future employment of youth. Each paper example shows how a category of aspects of SMEs can benefit our readers.

TABLE OF CONTENTS

SME INTRODUCTION: How We Think
by Eva Kras 0

SME Do we need a NEW ECONOMICS for
Sustainable Development?
by Peter Soderbaum. 0

SME Contributing to a CULTURE of
Multi-Generational Unity; Exercising your
Leadership to Connect in Extraordinary Ways
by Carolina Rekar Munro. 0

SME COMMUNITY Based Economics Development:
Learning from Employee Ownership and Social Enterprise:
by Darcy Hitchcock 0

SME The Value of Ecosystem Services
by Jacques Chirazi. 0

SME Approaching Emerging Issues
by Maria Teresa Bianchi,
Sapienza University of Rome, Italy. 0

SME "Alfa" and "OMEGA" for Development:
by Ineza Gagnidze, Irina Gogorishvili, Nino Papachashvili,
TBILIST State University, Georgia. 0

HOW WE THINK

Eva Kras

This first paper introduces the new world of the smaller business sector, including future thinking involving the basic needs for work for many present-day young people. This involves smaller organizations such as SMEs, cooperatives, and some NGOs, and is especially directed to the youth sector. Regarding the future, it deals with a period of approximately twenty to twenty-five years, looking into the future of business in many continents.

This introduction deals with a new way of thinking in business and at home. It provides some basic ideas for the reader who is looking for new thinking and the theories related to the development of small business for our future. This book will be followed by and closely connected to a second devoted to actual case studies from different countries, showing how these "new" ideas and a new way of thinking about business is already present in a small (and increasing) number of smaller companies.

As a result, this introduction deals fundamentally with "how we think" in business, and the advantage we now have in looking very closely at youth employment and youth concerns, which combine many aspects of present-day thinking, with new ideas for the future of their work and life in general.

New research has come to light within a subject that has been controversial for many years on many continents—how our brains work, aspects of right- and left-brain thinking (McGilchrist) and their relation to how we think about business today in many continents and cultures.

The papers in this book will show us different aspects of the "big picture" of development for the longer term and genuinely sustainable thinking for our future, and how business, in general, can improve for most people.

Welcome to this book, reader. We hope it will leave you with much new longer-term thinking and point toward important actions for each decade in the future.

OUR CURRENT CIRCUMSTANCES

For many years, especially in the Western world, we have established some principles or assumptions that we believe in as truths. These principles and their underlying views, related to how we think, have also formed the basis for all our institutions, governments, business sector, and civil society. This whole package is what we usually refer to as the essence of our accepted "conventional thinking."

In recent years we have begun to experience some worrisome ecological, social, and economic consequences of the practices and policies related to our conventional thinking. As a society, we have attempted to deal with these destructive consequences in a number of ways, which include:

1.) Changing some policies and practices to reflect concerns about some ecological and social issues, but without questioning our underlying conventional thinking base, on which these policies are seated. This has meant, for example, superimposing "sustainable"-sounding policies and practices on top of conventional principles and values. The outcomes have led to some short-term improvements but in general have proven disappointing.

2.) At the same time, few diverse, small-scale models of new "thinking" are emerging (like models to alleviate our ecological and social destruction) in many regions. As a result, we have seen positive outcomes in some areas, but when attempting to move these models into a bigger company region, many misunderstandings and controversies have resulted. These seem to be based on a "different way of thinking."

In light of these attempts, it appears something else is needed to bridge the gap between often good intentions on the one side and unfavorable outcomes on the other. In this process, we need to search for the roots of our misunderstandings and misinterpretations in organizations, across cultures, disciplines, and societal sectors.

We Are In Fact in the Middle of a Dilemma!

For a start, we urgently need to find a viable long-term solution to the worrisome growing destruction of our fragile ecological and social systems. And we do not have the luxury of time, as breakdowns are becoming very serious in some regions, and we are already in "overshoot" conditions in some areas, based on studies by specialists in the field.

At the same time, the social issues related mainly to humanity and how we think are also deeply affected but rarely taken seriously.

What Can We Do?

It appears that we need to search much deeper into the roots of our destructive behavior. We need to find principles for the long term that all humans in all organizations, disciplines, sectors, and cultures can relate to and agree upon in this interconnected world. This involves "how we think" in its broadest form. The author has sought the insights of a number of internationally respected visionaries. Their wisdom is key in our search for a viable long-term solution to our dilemma.

First, it appears we need to transform our way of thinking about our problems. This search takes us across a broad spectrum of areas, such as most business sectors, governments, and importantly, all levels of universities. This "rethinking" will be especially important for youth, who today are struggling with the concept of work (or lack of it) and the meaning of their lives.

This book is an attempt to provide new insights into some of the most complex aspects of our way of thinking about transformation, the values that control our way of thinking, how we view the future of our working lives, and the future we are leaving for the youth of today.

Most of us believe in a "sustainable" approach to life and work, where the goal is advancing the well-being of both people and the world ecosystems. We are accustomed to hearing and reading about many well-publicized government and business policies, which express their commitment to "sustainable development," in support of human and ecological well-being. And yet:

Why do we see so few concrete actions implemented for long-term improvements in human life and nature, in spite of the these expressed good intentions?

Facts Related to Our Present Development

1.) We live in a money-based society. When people judge whether society accepts them, money has become the first consideration. There are many explanations for this, including the needs of a new competitive society, in which "bigger is better" seems to be very important in business especially.
2.) Modern technologies have been proliferating but have eliminated many jobs, with no obvious hope for their replacement.
3.) We have seen environmental progress but still have far to go to build new jobs that will result from this whole new

world. Youth is especially affected. There seems to be a disconnect between good ecological budgeting and our accepted dependence on nature for our lives and our work.
4.) According to serious studies, for the first time in many generations, youth today appear to face a more difficult financial situation than previous generations. They are struggling to find work in most developed as well as developing countries.
5.) Young people, in general, are anxious to use their abilities in new ways, hence the growth of innovation—especially SMEs but also new cooperatives and some NGOs.
6.) The pressures to acquire "everything money can buy" as a ticket to societal acceptance is gradually reducing among youth, with more recognition and emphasis on the human thinking or "character" of an individual. This is a prolonged process.
7.) Ecological recognition and seriousness are coming to the fore. Even internationally, emphasis on these matters is becoming more urgent. Many countries have made some genuine progress, but they still use conventional thinking.
8.) We are gradually finding some new alternatives to conventional thinking. In some countries, youth especially are looking for alternative ways of thinking.

What We Need

1.) A new approach to the concept of success in everyday work: We need to question the now present importance for society of "money" as the important way of measuring even happiness, position in society and success.
2.) We need to find a solution to the overarching problem of thinking seriously about nature—and our limited world. We have obvious limitations in "conventional thinking."

3.) We need to find a viable solution for the realities of the human need for work, especially as it concerns our most vulnerable, our youth.

NEW THINKING: INFLUENCE OF RIGHT AND LEFT BRAIN

To begin this process, it seems that we all need to be "on the same page," so to speak, about how we think. Doing so can put us in a common place that makes us both successful and happy in our work as well as satisfied in life. Therefore, let us look at some of the most recent and breakthrough research on the subject.

Scientist and philosopher Iain McGilchrist put the results of a twenty-year study into an essential book for the business and educational world today, *The Master and His Emissary: The Divided Brain and the Making of the Modern World*. In this book, McGilchrist has informed us of new insights into the functioning of our brain, especially regarding right- and left-brain thinking. Much research has been done over the years regarding this subject, but now we can begin to answer some of our deepest questions related to how we think and what makes us truly happy in life and work.

We have treated left-brain thinking as dominant, especially in business, as almost all scientific research and accepted thinking relies on it. We have believed that the right brain should only be taken seriously in spiritual thinking, which is considered personal territory and thus better "left at home" when we are concerned with business logic and science.

Now that is changing, with the new research available, such as McGilchrist's work, regarding the incredible strength of our right brain—which applies to all humanity. This work is especially important today as we struggle with many problems that the conventional way of thinking does not seem to be able to handle. The right brain can see the "big picture" of life and work; thus, it appears to be instrumental in our long-term plans in life. And the innovative SME can absorb much of what the right brain is trying to teach us.

McGilchrist claims we should pay careful attention to our right hemisphere to "receive instructions" for all left-brain activities. The left brain is still important to us, however. The right brain can give us unprecedented, much-needed instructions in human, ecological, and deep-happiness areas, but there is one thing it cannot do. We need the left brain to put activities into practice that the right-brain "big picture" has shown us. Thus the left brain becomes an "Emissary," the part of the brain that puts the right brain ideas into practice.

This is quite shocking news in the left-brain-dominant world in which we live. And now we are learning that in fact, we should be thinking about and following the indications of the right brain's big picture, making humanity and nature as our prime concerns.

Are we turning over conventional thinking related to business in general? Are we saying that our old priorities—first economics, then ecology, then sociology—should shift to a different order—sociology/humanity, then ecology, then economics?

To look more deeply, we can recommend that you look at the thinking of some highly respected international thinkers, many of whom are or were important business executives. They all have shown very highly developed right- and left-brain thinking, and have all contributed much to our understanding of this new world of innovative thinking and SMEs, and thus provided keys to the future. For a start, we recommend Albert Einstein, Ervin Laszlo, David Korten, Hazel Henderson, and Iain McGilchrist.

New Thinking, Diagrammed

Following is a helpful table that shows the differences between conventional and genuine long-term sustainable development thinking.

HOW OUR BRAIN WORKS

CONVENTIONAL THINKING	
LEFT-BRAIN	RIGHT-BRAIN
Master of All Business and Planning	Spirituality
Master of All Societal Activities	Consciousness and Emotions
Logical/Rational Thinking Throughout, including Education	No Connections to Logical/Rational Thinking
Short-Term Thinking	Long-Term Thinking

GENUINE SUSTAINABLE THINKING	
LEFT-BRAIN	RIGHT-BRAIN
Accepts Position as Emissary of Right Brain Development "Big Picture" Thinking	Master of All "Big Picture"
Basis for Development of All Ideas: "Right Brain" Thinking	Expects Left Brain to Plan How to Put Big Picture Ideas into Practice
Right Brain Cannot Put Anything into Practice and Needs Left Brain to Do So	Spiritualtiy, Consciousness, and Emotion
Short-Term Thinking	Long-Term Thinking

Overall, this compares two types of thinking and lets us understand our present confusion. We have relied on left-brain thinking only and are now learning to appreciate right-brain thinking for this new transformation viewed in SMEs. The wonderful thing about this is that we all have both sides in our human brain from birth but have been relying on only the left brain for all our questions and answers. Now we have an opportunity at the local community level to make this improvement in rethinking our whole lives!

NEW PARADIGMS FOR OUR NEW WORLD OF BUSINESS

Now let us look at some simple examples of how this change in thinking will affect our everyday thinking and how this process will affect our new world of business.

CONVENTIONAL THINKING	NEW THINKING IN SME
LEFT-BRAIN THINKING	RIGHT-BRAIN THINKING
a.) Competition	a.) Sharing
b.) Money Based Society	b.) Human Relations and Nature
c.) Economics Priority	c.) Modest Income Social/ Ecological area
d.) Emphasis on Large Companies	d.) Emphasis on SME, Humanit, and Nature
e.) Strong Individualism	e.) Strong Communal Good (cooperation)

What do these above points in this comparison mean?

Competition Vs. Sharing

Competition: The concept of competitiveness ensures that we view other people and companies as competitors. We are also careful even with allies. We should be concerned about telling them as little as possible (for fear they may want to steal our ideas). We learn not to trust them with any knowledge that may be useful for their company or negative for us. Left-brain thinking alone is paramount.

Sharing: With right-brain usage, we trust others. We feel good about sharing and are convinced it can help both parties. Examples of this are viewed in SMEs.

In small companies, we welcome sharing information in place of competing with others. The idea is we trust others and feel deeply that sharing information with others will be helpful in work and life for both sides. The thought of competition leads to distrust and separates humans in place of bringing them closer to each other. It is outside basic concepts of the new right-brain way of thinking.

Money-Based Society Versus Human Relations and Nature

Money: Purely left-brain thinkers are mostly always concerned about the power of money. We have become accustomed to a society where "money rules," and we try our best to do things which show our values based on it. The organization and the shareholders hold principles in common that steer any business plans or mission. These standards must be adhered to by all. We respect and admire money and people who have it. We see our jobs and society in terms of money, which controls everything around us.

Human Relations and Nature: On the contrary, right-brain people (SME workers, for example), who see the "big picture," are concerned about two main items: our humanity and what is best for MOST people, plus nature around us, which really controls everything we can do, today and especially in the future. We depend on nature and our own bodies for any plans we make. This calls for developing the new, right-brain priorities. SMEs are likewise worried about human factors and nature. Communities form the "glue that keeps people together and thinking the same way."

Economic Priority Vs. Modest Income

Economic Priority: This involves the money factors associated with left-brain thinking, as is the situation today. This economic factor remains the biggest factor in all activities.

Modest Income: Innovative SMEs are looking for a modest income, but at the same time want to "have a life" aside from work. There is also an emphasis on overall happiness in work, families, and communities. Nature also plays a key role in all people's planning.

New right-brain thinking changes society's priorities completely, from economics to humanity, genuine ecological concerns, and participation. People and nature are so important that these relationships become crucial, and economic expectations are lowered—and workers are happy with this. This concept then becomes a societal standard of importance, and people begin to value families more, good friends more, and value human relationships more. They also look long-term at ecological areas and act differently. They think seriously about what they are leaving for their children and offspring in general. Selfishness in their own lives transforms into realistic thinking about the next generation. They tend to think: "Do they not deserve the same or better possibilities than what we received?"

Emphasis on Large International Agreements vs.
Emphasis on Small Companies and Trust

International Agreements: Worldwide, society is focused on "bigger is better," even though that philosophy benefits only a small sector of people financially and splits up communities around the world. This results in loss of jobs and culture and "belonging." It also serves to "homogenize" our tastes as much as possible. Imagine a world where everyone wears blue jeans.

International agreements usually depend on a lot of money. Much of that money pays for lawyers to interpret the laws of each country involved and compare them with our own.

What happens when a country has laws which are based on a different set of principles from our own? Suppose our own country is based on a massive number of laws which hopefully cover almost every situation that arises, and a foreign country has a legal system based on a set of principles (human and ecological) within which they work, which covers all situations related to their country? Then we have a new problem, as these principles need to be understood across cultures. Lawyers are often confused by this concept of principle-based legal systems, and it can often create problems where interpretations differ.

SMEs and Trust: On the other hand, innovative SMEs tend to value humanity in general. Trust flows, and community strength becomes very important, as the innovative SME sector becomes a strong part of the community and strengthens it with belief in humanity.

Today, taking into account the new right-brain thinking, a big consideration is trust. When humanity and nature are the most important, we naturally develop trust as a key to getting along with people of a different culture. Money as such is not the most important factor. It is now closely involved with a common agreement related to humanity and ecological considerations. Trust comes with that—money will always be part of the process, but is not a question of "who gets the best part of any agreement."

Strong Individualism Vs. Common Good and Cooperation

Strong Individualism: Strong individualism has become even stronger as businesses grow bigger. People in a large company must sincerely place business interests first in all they do every day, as part of their job. But something seems to be left out.

What happens when so many friends lose their jobs even though the large business is advertised as a success story for all, even though the winners as such in a money-based society demonstrate strong individualism?

Who really wins and who loses?

These are areas that usually concern both sides of any agreement, as each has different values that come forth—one is extreme individualism, especially involved in the owners, and the money culture and the other is concerned about humanity, nature, and the future.

Common Good and Cooperation: Innovative SMEs have humanity as a mainstay, and thus community needs and development become important. Cooperatives have also grown as a natural place for people to cooperate, to feel trust, and to work with trust, as they take the whole person into account.

People who believe in the new world in general always seem to place more importance on the "common good" than on individualism. This is a huge difference, one that has divided many countries and cultures in our modern world. It often sabotages agreements, as most in society today want to win financially, especially the few at the top of an organization. Strong individualism has provided for many generations, and now we have a world which has created the ultimate individualism, in which individualism comes together with money.

Think differently, and with the "common good," communities enter a period of strength, with many new jobs, and people in power are more concerned about humanity and nature, not individualism. Trust in people becomes the final result. Service to the community becomes a huge responsibility as the "common good," and helping others becomes a service to the community.

WELCOME TO THE NEW WORLD OF THINKING!

In summary, the following values and developments help to make innovative SMEs a viable future for many parts of the world. Therefore we need to begin to accept right-brain thinking as a priority in our thinking and accept left-brain thinking as important to put right-brain "big picture" ideas into action.

1.) Community becomes a new theme, as innovative SMEs become an important part of a community.
2.) Personal human qualities, such as trust, belonging, cooperation, and modest income, become positive feelings about humanity and thus also our ecological reality.
3.) Helping others—often not expecting anything in return—provides the basis for a small, daily, positive action every day that helps to make us all feel a depth of happiness each day.

Welcome to a new world of thinking!

We are entering a new world for the future, where humans and nature become central to all the work we do. We can then accept that our right-brain thinking is essential to bring about this huge change in our way of thinking and working. Hopefully, the world of youth will become central to this new world. They now have new hope for their future!

A NEW ECONOMICS FOR SUSTAINABLE DEVELOPMENT

Peter Söderbaum

When asked about the "economic" aspect of an activity or project people tend to think about "money." Focus on this monetary or financial aspect is broadly in line with neoclassical economic theory, the conceptual framework taught at university departments of economics in different parts of the world. Economics is defined as the allocation of or "management of scarce resources" (Mankiw, 2011, p. 2) where optimal solutions are normally explored in monetary terms. This neoclassical theory includes two actor categories: consumers (or households) and firms. Consumers and firms interact in three kinds of markets: for commodities, for labor, and for financial capital. It is assumed consumers maximize utility within the scope of their monetary budget while firms maximize monetary profits. At the macro or national level, gross domestic product, a specific summary of all market transactions, is the main progress indicator. For preparing investments in roads, airports, energy systems, and other infrastructure projects, neoclassical theory advocates cost-benefit analysis (CBA) in monetary terms.

Neoclassical assumptions have certainly had an impact upon the cognitive habits of individuals as consumers, of business leaders, politicians, and governmental administrators. In some sense, consumers may feel that they are successful in maximizing utility. Business leaders may be successful in terms of monetary profits. At issue is whether such thinking patterns are appropriate in the present situation. Sustainable development or sustainability is one of the current challenges. Although neoclassical theory has something to offer even regarding sustainable development, it may be a limited theoretical framework. Rather than the current neoclassical monopoly, we need competition. Rather than thinking in terms of paradigm shift (Kuhn, 1970), we need to think in terms of paradigm coexistence (Söderbaum, 2000, pp. 29–30) and pluralism.

Neoclassical theory at the micro and macro levels has influenced thinking patterns in a period when development has become unsustainable in many ways. Climate change is one example; loss of biological diversity and pollution of air, water, and soil are others. While we should not exclude neoclassical ideas, it is a bit strange to argue that we in the present situation should exclusively listen to advocates of a theory that has failed in relation to sustainability. We also need to test other theoretical perspectives in economics. Can they improve our chances of dealing with sustainability and other issues?

REDEFINING ECONOMICS IN TERMS OF ULTIDIMENSIONAL ANALYSIS AND DEMOCRACY

A proposed new theoretical perspective starts with a partly different definition of economics: "Economics is the multidimensional management of (limited) resources in a democratic society."

Why "multidimensional" management? Multidimensionality goes against the one-dimensional analysis of neoclassical theory and method. "Monetary reductionism" is no longer accepted. The idea that we should put a monetary price on all impacts, ecosystem services included, to make them commensurable and tradeable, is abandoned. Instead, analysis keeps implications of different kinds separate throughout analysis. One considers non-monetary impacts to be as "economic" as monetary ones. This may make analysis more complex but also more relevant. Sweden has proposed sixteen environmental objectives to monitor the quality and state of the environment as well as possible (Swedish Environmental Agency, 2016). At the UN level, world leaders agreed about eight Millennium Development Goals in the year 2000. This process of broadening the agenda has continued with seventeen Sustainable Development Goals (SDGs) sanctioned by the UN in November 2015. They are:

- No poverty
- Zero hunger
- Good health and well-being
- Quality education
- Gender equality
- Clean water and sanitation
- Affordable and clean energy
- Decent work and economic growth
- Industry, innovation, and infrastructure
- Reduced inequalities
- Sustainable cities and communities
- Responsible consumption and production
- Climate action
- Life below water
- Life on land
- Peace, justice, and strong institutions
- Partnerships to reach goals

The UN further elaborated each set of goals including some sub-goals and targets to be achieved in the next fifteen years: "For the goals to be reached, everyone needs to do their part: government, the private sector, civil society and people like you" (United Nations, Sustainable Development Knowledge Platform, 2016).

The above list of objectives points to a disaggregated and multidimensional view of sustainable development. One dimensional aggregation in monetary or other terms does not appear meaningful. Economic growth in traditional terms is part of the list but only one of the seventeen SDGs. Performance of the goals is an issue for all individuals in all potentially relevant roles. This suggests that we need to abandon the neoclassical mechanistic idea of individuals and organizations in favor of a view where actors are responsible and accountable. To this, we will return.

Why the reference to a democratic society? When one reads neoclassical introductory textbooks in economics, it becomes clear that "democracy" is not a theme taken seriously. These texts rather emphasize economists as experts, calling for a kind of technocracy. In Mankiw and Taylor, "democracy" is not even part of the index or glossary. But democracy should play a crucial role at two levels:

- Regarding the discipline of economics itself. We should not accept neoclassical monopoly or dictatorship.
- Regarding our understanding of individuals as actors in the economy. We should respect that individuals differ in values and ideological orientation.

A proposed new theoretical perspective starts with a partly different definition of economics: "Economics is the multidimensional management of (limited) resources in a democratic society."

Economics as a discipline is in need of democratization (Söderbaum and Brown, 2010). As scholars, we should admit that a specific paradigm (theoretical perspective) in economics is not only theory; it is also specific in value or ideological terms. Gunnar Myrdal, a well-known institutional economist, argues that "values are always with us" (Myrdal, 1973, 1978) in the different stages of the research process from the formulation of problems to the presentation of results. Neoclassical theory is specific in ideological terms with its focus on markets and the monetary dimension. Applying Economic-Man assumptions and looking at organizations in profit-maximizing terms are other examples. The reasons for some of us economists to look for different theoretical perspectives are not only scientific (in some narrow sense) but also ideological. Those of us who claim to take environmental issues seriously and advocate institutional environmental (or ecological) economics as alternative perspective do so for scientific as well as ideological reasons.

If there are options at the level of ideology, then democracy becomes important also when understanding individuals in the economy and respecting differences in their ideological orientations. Neoclassical economists, with their CBAs, claim expertise in "correct values" in market terms for purposes of assessing impacts of investments in infrastructure. They claim the ability to identify the best or optimal solution for society as a whole among competing investment projects. Applying positional analysis (PA) as an alternative method means that we in many situations have to refer to conditional conclusions rather than one single optimal solution. Alternative investment projects will be ranked differently, depending on the ideological orientation considered. And in many decision situations, it is not realistic to assume that all stakeholders and concerned actors share the same idea about what is progress in society. Such ideas may differ between political parties in a democratic society, for example.

OVERVIEW OF DIFFERENCES BETWEEN NEOCLASSICAL AND INSTITUTIONAL ECONOMICS

The left-hand column of Table 1 shows the essential elements of neoclassical economic theory. I have chosen to point to the view of the individual, the organization, and the market, as well as ideas about institutional change, progress in society, and approach to sustainability assessment. In the right-hand column, I have identified corresponding views and concepts of institutional theory as parts of an alternative perspective.

Table 1. Differences between neoclassical and institutional economics

	NEOCLASSICAL ECONOMICS	INSTITUTIONAL ECONOMICS
Individual	Economic Man	Political Economic Person (PEP)
Organization	Profit-maximizing firm	Political Economic Organization (PEO)
Market	Mechanistic ideas of supply and demand	PEPs and PEOs as Market Actors, Relationships, and Networks
Institutional Change	Change in Regulation of Market Incentives	Also Actor-Network Approach
Progress Indicatiors	Gross Domestic Product (GDP) (Side Concern: Employment)	Open Issue where Sustainable Development Goals (SDGs) are Part
Approach to Sustanability Assessment	Cost-Benefit Analysis (CBA)	Positional Analysis (PA)

The role of values and ideology in economics suggests that economics is always "political economics." The individual as a political economic person (PEP) is "an actor guided by her ideological orientation." Ideological orientation is something that differs between individuals; some bother more than others about threats of climate change for example. Such differences are of relevance in economic analysis.

A political economic organization (PEO) is similarly an actor guided by its "ideological orientation" or "mission." Business corporations or firms is only one category of organizations, and the role of monetary profits or other financial considerations is partly an open issue. The debate about corporate social responsibility (CSR) is an example of this. It is worth studying the differences between business leaders and other actors in organizations in relation to sustainable development.

Rather than the mechanistic view of markets in neoclassical theory, a focus will be on the behavior of individuals as market actors. Institutional theory understands actors in terms of social psychology and refers to an actor's ideological orientation, which is not limited to self-interest. Each market actor is related to other market actors in supply chains and networks.

When institutional change is concerned, neoclassical economists tend to point to incentive systems in monetary market terms. Taxes and environmental charges are examples. As an institutional economist, I am a bit skeptical of such proposals. Inherent in neoclassical ideology is a fundamental belief that interventions in existing markets are generally dysfunctional. I see changes in institutional arrangements more as a result of a power game between different actors. State intervention is an option where taxes and monetary incentives can play important roles, but voluntary action is also possible.

We have already touched on GDP as an indicator of progress. This indicator suffers from the aforementioned "monetary reductionism," and the recent emphasis at the international level on seventeen SDGs is thus an important step forward. For sustainability assessment, neoclassical economists recommend CBA, which reduces all kinds of impacts to their alleged monetary equivalents. An ambitious study of ecosystem services and biodiversity where the United Nations Environmental Program (UNEP) played an important role, the so-called TEEB-study, is an example of this (Kumar, ed., 2010). I have elsewhere discussed this study (2013, 2015). There are alternatives to CBA, and my preference is positional analysis (PA), an approach based on the multidimensional and disaggregated idea of economics previously discussed.

THE CONCEPTS OF DEMOCRACY AND IDEOLOGICAL ORIENTATION

In a democratic society, there are normally different political parties, each with an ideology or ideological orientation. Actors belonging to specific political parties try to convince citizens (or actors in other roles) with their ideas. And citizens respond in some way, suggesting that they too are guided by a kind of ideological orientation.

Moving societies from present unsustainable tendencies in a green or more sustainable direction is a matter not exclusively of science and management but also of ideology. And just as there are ideological orientations that downplay climate change and other sustainability concerns, there are also competing views about how to best transform society in a "green" direction.

Green issues compete with other issues in the brains and thinking patterns of actors. There are capacity limits for dialogue in different arenas, such as specific newspapers. Climate change appears as an urgent issue for many of us, but does it get the priority it deserves? These days, public debate is focused on the war in Syria, and to my knowledge, there are not many attempts to systematically relate these destructive activities to climate change or the seventeen SDGs previously listed.

Democracy stands for a political system where it is possible to raise various concerns or issues to make them part of actors' agendas in various arenas. Democracy is not only a system of voting rules in parliamentary elections. It is also about human rights such as freedom of speech, freedom of association, and generally a willingness to listen to actors with an ideological orientation that differs from your own (as long as these voices do not go against democracy itself). Actors who differ in views can learn from each other, suggesting that democracy can contribute to creative outcomes of public dialogue. In this sense, democracy can be part of the security system of a society. Moving from it toward dictatorship would reduce security.

Democracy versus dictatorship is not a simple matter of either-or. Democratic elements can be identified in a society described as a dictatorship, and democracy can always be strengthened in countries such as Canada or Sweden. The world and all its nations have institutions protecting mainstream interests. The monopoly of neoclassical economic theory at university departments of economics is a case in point. Even institutions such as the Bank of Sweden's Nobel Prize in Economic Sciences make the transformation to sustainability more difficult by systematically protecting the neoclassical paradigm. This neoclassical perspective legitimizes the present political system legitimate in a situation where institutional change is needed.

There are different theories of democracy. Some assume it aims at a consensus that is obtainable through dialogue. There is certainly a need for many kinds of agreement at local, national, regional, and global levels, but like Chantal Mouffe (2005, 2013), I tend to believe that democracy is also and perhaps primarily about how to live with disagreement. Aiming always at consensus risks neglecting or even eliminating those with a different opinion. This is what happens, for example, in the international dialogue (or lack of it) about economics where the mentioned Economics Prize plays a role. In some nations today, Turkey being a possible example, attempts to eliminate opposition can hardly be regarded as compatible with democracy.

Ideology is a "contested concept" (Connolly, 1974) in that it can be understood in more ways than one. *Power, institution, democracy,* and *value* are other contested concepts relevant to social science. When using concepts of this kind, one has to clarify their meaning as well as possible. I here discuss ideology and ideological orientation in means-ends terms. They are about where you are (original position), where you want to go (future positions) and how to get there (strategy).

The ideological orientation of an actor varies more or less over time with situation and context. While neoclassical economists refer to objective mathematical functions and optimal solutions in precise terms, an ideological orientation is often fragmentary and uncertain.

It can furthermore be narrow or broad. It can reflect self-interest but also ideas about common interests or concerns for future generations. Ideological orientation in this sense points in the same direction as Herman Daly's reference to "the common good" (Daly and Cobb, 1989). Reference to "the" common good may suggest there is one single idea of common interests. In a democracy, there are—as we have argued—competing varieties of ideological orientation and thereby competing ideas of the meaning of "common good."

Whether expressed in quantitative, qualitative, visual terms or some combination thereof, an actor's ideological orientation can guide behavior and investment decisions. In what way? This can be understood as a "matching" process where an actor matches their own multidimensional and multifaceted ideological orientation against the multidimensional impact profile of each alternative of choice considered. They look for an alternative with expected impacts that match their ideological orientation as well as possible. Reference can also be made to "compatibility," "appropriateness," or "pattern recognition." E. F. Schumacher pointed to the need for "appropriate technology" at an early stage in his book (1973), and pattern recognition is a term closer to computer language. Ideological orientation, as *Small is Beautiful* well as expected impacts connected with specific alternatives, can be understood in terms of patterns.

RECONSIDERING "COSTS" AND "BENEFITS"

Neoclassical analysis interprets costs and benefits in monetary or financial terms. A case in point is neoclassical cost-benefit analysis (CBA). The idea is that only that counts which can be quantified, and a way of achieving this is to put price tags on all kinds of impacts. However, actors may assume that an impact has been fully considered when a monetary price has been chosen. Non-monetary impacts somehow disappear from analysis to become invisible.

A way of dealing with this is to keep monetary and non-monetary impacts separate and use the terms of "cost" and "benefit" both on the monetary and non-monetary side (Table 2). Non-monetary costs and benefits (B and D in Table 2) are regarded as important as such and not reducible to monetary impacts. The importance of impacts in a decision becomes an issue of the knowledge available to an actor, their specific situation, and their ideological orientation.

Table 2. Classification of costs and benefits in economic analysis

	MONETARY	NON-MONETARY
Cost	A	B
Benefit	C	D

In the case of constructing a motorway where there are agricultural land and forest with connected ecosystems, the CB-analyst tends to focus on construction costs in financial terms. Buying the area needed is one part of the financial outlays and paying the construction company another part. But does this covers the whole "cost?" Agricultural land and forests become asphalt surface, suggesting more or less irreversible losses in ecosystem function. Irreversible losses are hardly measurable in monetary terms. And where does the asphalt come from?

One way of understanding what happens in non-monetary terms is to think about how options for future decisions are affected. A new road will increase opportunities for those using it for transportation purposes, but the transformation from agricultural land to asphalt surface is largely irreversible. Some farms may close down, and the farmers look upon monetary and non-monetary impacts in their own way. The important thing for the decision-maker is to know what she is doing in multidimensional terms and for whom.

When dealing with inertia (in its different forms) and future options, it becomes relevant to distinguish between impacts' "flows" and "positions" (Table 3). On the monetary side, the turnover of a company exemplifies a monetary flow (E in Table 3) while financial assets and debts at a point in time are examples of monetary positions. When non-monetary impacts are concerned, CO2 emissions from transportation activities per year are a flow, whereas the size of land used for transportation purposes in a city at a point in time is a non-monetary position.

Table 3. A classification of impacts in terms of flows and positions

	FLOW (referring to a period of time)	POSITION (referring to a point in time)
Monetary	E	F
Non-monetary	G	H

Positional analysis (PA) is an approach to sustainability assessment that considers monetary as well as non-monetary impact but emphasizes non-monetary flows and positions (or states). It argues that sustainability impact studies, monitoring, and accounting systems should focus much more (than in CBA) on such non-monetary aspects.

PA is described elsewhere (Söderbaum, 2000, Brown et al., 2017). Its purpose is to illuminate an issue in a many-sided way concerning relevant ideological orientations, alternatives of choice and impacts. It furthermore tries to identify conflicts of interest and make them visible (rather than assume all stakeholders and concerned actors agree on one single objective function as in CBA). Conclusions regarding ranking the alternatives considered are conditional about each ideological orientation considered. PA then claims to be an approach to decision-making compatible with the essential features of democracy. At an early stage, the analyst also enters into a problem-solving dialogue with stakeholders, others concerned, and decision-makers.

INDIVIDUALS AND ORGANIZATIONS AS POLITICAL ACTORS

The neoclassical approach to environmental and sustainability problems can be described as follows. It is believed that markets on their own automatically can handle many kinds of problems in the economy and that they generally stand for efficiency. A first recommendation is, therefore, to refrain from "unnecessary government intervention." But neoclassical economists understand that there are what they see as exceptions, where markets can fail and harm an environment. They then refer to externalities: single impacts on third parties (outside the market transaction). The third party suffers but can be compensated in monetary terms according to the "polluter-pays principle." There is also an idea of how the correct compensation can be estimated. Neoclassical economists (with their neoliberal agenda) are eager to point out that governments can also fail by subsidizing activities in the economy that are harmful to the environment. Such subsidies, it is argued, should be removed.

Institutional economists such as William Kapp (1970, Berger and Steppacher, eds 2011) do not see environmental impacts as single disturbances in a system that otherwise is functioning well. Environmental impacts connected with production, trade, and transportation are ubiquitous and corporations tend to systematically eliminate monetary costs by carrying over environmental harm to society at large (just as many corporations do what they can to avoid paying taxes that would, when paid, make it easier for local and national governments to deal with environmental and other problems).

Or, in the words of William Kapp himself: "Thus, a system of decision-making, operating in accordance with the principle of investment for profit, cannot be expected to proceed in any other way but to try to reduce its costs whenever possible by shifting them to the shoulders of others or to society at large" (Kapp, 1970, p. 18).

From a neoclassical perspective, policy and politics are in the hands of national and local governments. My view of policy and politics as institutionalist is much broader. Each individual and organization is a potential and actual policymaker, as suggested by the concepts "political economic person" and "political economic organization." All actors contribute to aggravate or improve the environment (and other sustainability indicators in positional terms). Each actor has their rights and responsibilities in a democratic society.

Individuals as actors relate to each other in networks. Based on their ideological orientations or missions, they interact—cooperate or compete—with other actors. One problem is that our political-economic system, with all its institutions, does not easily change. Inertia and path dependence makes it difficult to turn the economy and society from its present unsustainable path to one which is more sustainable. Some powerful individuals and organizations as actors. For example, transnational corporations furthermore protect institutional arrangements (and may work for institutional change in an even more unsustainable direction).

In this situation where a transformation is needed but where there are many kinds of inertia, all actors are important, but some are perhaps more important than others. Eva Kras (2007), former president of the Canadian Society for Ecological Economics, has repeatedly argued that we need to listen to "visionaries," actors who tend to face fundamental scientific and ideological issues rather than avoid them. The visionaries play an important role, but so do also all those open-minded enough to listen to voices outside the mainstream. There are visionaries within science but also among other actors in the broad public dialogue about progress in society.

While many individuals qualify as visionaries, I will here only single out two early and two more recent visionaries in the debate about the future of our societies. E. F. Schumacher, I0 have already mentioned. In his book, he reminds us that "small is beautiful" and that there is a need for an economics "as if people mattered." Smallholders may be successful in many ways, and dimensions and neoclassical ideas about "economies of scale" are too simplistic.

A second early writer is Hazel Henderson, whose collected writings, published in *Creating Alternative Futures. The End of Economics* (1980) still seems relevant today. However, I understand her subtitle "The End of Economics" as directed to the neoclassical mainstream rather than all kinds of economics. Henderson is worried about "creeping gigantism" (p. 163) and the power of transnational corporations when compared with smallholders and other small companies. In her view "the reliance on global price mechanisms blinded economists" to mounting environmental and ecological problems" (p. 3). She also refers to the "bankruptcy of economics" (p. 4). In more positive terms, she points to a large number of examples of an "emerging counter-economy" (pp. 381–389) from UN conferences dealing with different issues to local initiatives.

More recent writings by visionaries include Naomi Klein's book *This Changes Everything. Capitalism vs. the Climate* (2014) and George Monbiot's *How did we get into this mess? Politics, Equality, Nature* (2016). Klein points to the abuse of power of oil companies in relation to other interests, for example, those of indigenous people. Monbiot, a columnist for *The Guardian,* is attempting to bring issues into the political agenda where establishment actors tend to be silent.

This reference to some visionaries is of course not meant to do justice to their writings (and even less to the writings of all other visionaries) but should mainly serve to remind us that there is a danger in being limited to mainstream arguments and mainstream literature.

THE CASE OF "FREE TRADE" AGREEMENTS: CETA AND TTIP

Individuals like authors can act as precursors. But so can business companies, local governments, cities, universities, civil society organizations and even nations and groups of nation-states, such as the European Union. The opposite is also possible: they can delay necessary change. Let us look at proposed free trade agreements, such as CETA (Comprehensive Economic and Trade Agreement) between Canada and the European Union (EU) and TTIP (Transatlantic Trade and Investment Partnership) between USA and EU. A long period of negotiations is now followed by a period when contracts are supposed to be signed.

There is a mainstream in economics telling us that free international trade is good and attempts to protect home industry from competition are bad. "Protectionism" through tariffs and quotas is bad, and both nations benefit if such obstacles are reduced or eliminated. These recommendations are built upon simplistic neoclassical economics which have little to do with the complexities of the real world.

Neoclassical theory about international trade is, at the same time, ideology. This ideology has been internalized through economic education and in other ways by a large number of actors in society. The theory more precisely plays a role in making neoliberalism legitimate. It is not possible here to discuss all the assumptions behind the theory of international trade. There is an assumption, however, about homogenous commodities: that the same goods or services can be produced in both of the trading countries. This is seldom the case in reality. There is also an assumption that the interests of each nation can be dealt with in one-dimensional terms. In fact, there usually are conflicts of interest in each of the trading countries, such as those between labor interests and shareholder interests or between consumer interests and producer interests. One can only reduce conflicts of interest to one interest by choosing an ideological position. Environmental impacts and other externalities are peripheral to or outside of international trade theory. International trade in goods necessarily involves transportation, which leads to CO2 emissions. How can such impacts be assumed away today, when we claim to understand what we are doing to the climate?

A more realistic perspective on international trade in goods and services would suggest that "protectionism" often plays a positive role. Each country has an Environmental Protection Agency with the objective to protect ecosystems and natural resources. Today, reference is increasingly made to a need to "protect the planet," and why should those who think in such terms apologize? Similarly, there are national and international institutions with the purpose to protect human health. Transnational corporations prefer one system of health standards or environmental standards globally (which is stable over time) while some actors in a nation may prefer to control its standards and make changes in them when needed.

Included in the present negotiations is a kind of conflict resolution mechanism, ISDS (investor-state dispute settlement), which attributes a right to corporations to sue nations if their monetary profits are reduced by changes in national policy, for example, environmental policy or health policy. This is about not so-called free trade but protectionism of business interests. From a democratic point of view, this is a grotesque proposal. Should civil society organizations get a right to sue transnational corporations in a court of justice (built on principles at their own choice), if they feel that their interests threatened?

This is where we return to the possible role of nations, or parts of nations, as leaders in sustainability policy making. There is a neoliberal mainstream of actors on both sides of the Atlantic, but also numerous actors with a critical attitude. Among regions within the EU, Wallonia, an independent part of Belgium in some respects, protested and wanted to use their veto but finally were convinced by Cecilia Malmström, commissioner for international trade agreements in the EU, and others to accept. Malmström is a Liberal politician, and it is clear that the ideological orientation of the EU mainstream is neoliberal. The handling of this trade issue is an indicator of the strength of the mainstream and the ignorance by mainstream actors of other ways of thinking. Things are not finally settled yet, however, and one can hope that other regions and entities will follow the example of Wallonia in its arguments.

International trade theory does not deal with power issues and the ideological orientation of various actors. Mainstream economics textbooks hardly if ever mention the role of transnational corporations in the global economy. Free trade in the sense of tariffs and quotas already exists for many commodities, suggesting that cheap products in monetary terms are already available. Some of us may argue that some products are *too* cheap when considering the exploitation of cheap labor and other ways of lowering monetary costs. Further moves toward free trade are mainly a financial interest of big transnational corporations. These corporations want to dictate the rules of the game. But again joint stock companies are defined in reductionist, monetary, financial terms while present challenges are non-monetary, including the seventeen UN sanctioned SDGs previously discussed. Does this mean that joint stock companies are misconstructed in relation to present needs? I tend to think so. We need a debate about different forms of organization and their possible roles in society.

CONCLUSIONS FOR SUSTAINABILITY POLITICS

When asked about present unsustainable trends and how to transform them in a more sustainable direction, many would probably point to what they perceive as concrete issues, such as climate change, and then list various ways of reducing CO_2 emissions. In the present essay, I have argued that while such efforts are certainly desirable, we should also focus on perspectives, such as the neoclassical theory's close-to-monopoly position in the field of economics and the dominance of neoliberalism in politics. In fact, these issues are fundamental in dealing with present problems. It is an illusion that there can be value-free or value-neutral economics (von Egan-Krieger, 2014) and therefore we need to study and acknowledge the values or ideological orientation of each kind of economics. Just as neoclassical theory is close to neoliberalism, this essay's theory claims to be closer to a green or sustainability ideology where, for example, the seventeen SDGs play an essential role.

Rather than exclusively connecting sustainability policy and politics with government action and intervention in the economy, I have suggested that each individual in their own role is a policymaker. The individual as an actor is invited to participate in a dialogue about the future by listening to various, often contradictory voices. It is no longer enough to listen to those who claim expertise and act accordingly, since experts may—as in the case of economics—be "disciplinary monopolists" whose primary interest appears to be to protect the monopoly. This is a case of negative protectionism, but there are also positive examples of protectionism as we have argued. It should be added that it is not even enough to listen to various scientists. Sometimes it is important to listen to visionaries and to encourage scientists to do the same. And there are many other influential actors to bring into this dialogue, such as journalists, business leaders, actors from civil society organizations and politicians.

An alternative to neoclassical theory has to be built from the very beginning with a new or complementary definition of the subject. I have chosen to emphasize multidimensionality and democracy. Alternative views of individuals, organizations, markets, institutional change, sustainability assessment would then follow, as indicated in this essay and elsewhere (Söderbaum, 2016, 2017). But some ecological economists hold a partly different view (Costanza et al., 2017). Neoclassical economists resist radical change but may modify their arguments. "Natural capital" has become a key concept for some, comparable to social capital, human capital, and built capital (Helm, 2015). But these concepts are met with criticism, for example, by Richard Smith in the book *Green Capitalism. The God that failed* (2016).

Economists, in particular the neoclassical ones, claim expertise in forecasting while often failing to predict in practice. But other kinds of forecasting may be easier. Let me, therefore, predict that the debate about economics, ideology, and sustainability will continue in the future. At some stage, there will hopefully be a break-through with a more pluralist economics education and research at university departments of economics. Ideas about how such a change can take place exist in books (e.g., Madi and Reardon, 2014) as well as journals (e.g., *International Journal of Pluralism and Economics Education*).

REFERENCES

Berger, Sebastian & Rolf Steppacher, 2011. *The Foundations of Institutional Economics*. K. William Kapp. Routledge, London.

Brown, Judy, Malgorzata Dereniowska, Peter Söderbaum, 2017. *Positional Analysis for Sustainable Development: Reconsidering policy, economics, and accounting*. Routledge, London.

Connolly, William E., 1974, 1983. *The Terms of Political Discourse*. Blackwell, Oxford.

Costanza, Robert, Gar Alperovitz, Herman Daly, Joshua Farley, Carol Franco, Tim Jackson, Ida Kubiszewski, Juliet Schor & Peter Victor, 2017. Chapter 16, pp. 367–454 in Stanislav Shmelev, Ed. *Green Economy Reader: Lectures in Ecological Economics and Sustainability*. Springer International Publisher Switzerland AG.

Daly, Herman E. & John E. Cobb, 1989. *For the Common Good. Redirecting the Economy Toward Community, the Environment and a Sustainable Future*. Beacon Press, Boston.

von Egan-Krieger, Tanja, 2014. *Die Illusion wertfreier Ökonomie: Eine Untersuchung der Normativität heterodoxer Theorien*. Campus Verlag, Frankfurt.

Helm, Dieter, 2015. Natural Capital. *Valuing the planet*. Yale University Press, London.

Henderson, Hazel, 1980. *Creating Alternative Futures: The End of Economics*. Perigee Books, New York.

Kapp, K. William, 1970. *Environmental Disruption: General Issues and Methodological Problems*, Social Science Information (International Social Council), Vol. 4, No. 9, pp. 15–32.

Klein, Naomi, 2014. *This Changes Everything: Capitalism vs. the Climate.* Allen Lane, London.

Kras, Eva, 2007. *The Blockage: Rethinking Organizational Principles for the 21st Century.* American Literary Press, Chicago.

Kuhn, Thomas S., 1970. *The structure of scientific revolutions* (Second edition). Chicago University Press, Chicago.

Kumar, Pushpam, ed., 2010. *The Economics of Ecosystems and Biodiversity. Ecological and Economic Foundations* (The TEEB-study). Earthscan, London.

Madi, Maria Alejandra & Jack Reardon, 2014. *The Economics Curriculum: Toward a Radical Reformulation.* World Economics Association (WEA) Book Series Volume 1. College Publications (on behalf of WEA). Available at: www.worldeconomicsassociation.org

Mankiw, N. Gregory & Mark P. Taylor, 2011. *Economics.* Gengage Learning, Andover.

Monbiot, George, 2016. *How did we get into this mess? Politics, equality, nature.* Verso, London.

Mouffe, Chantal, 2005. *On the Political.* Routledge, London.

Mouffe, Chantal, 2013. *Agonistics: Thinking the World Politically.* Verso, London.

Myrdal, Gunnar, 1973. *Against the Stream: Critical Essays on Economics.* Random House, New York.

Myrdal, Gunnar, 1978. Institutional Economics. Journal of Economic Issues, Vol. 12, No. 4, pp. 771–783.

Schumacher, E. F., 1973. *Small is Beautiful: Economics as if People Mattered.* Harper & Row, New York.

Smith, Richard, 2016. *Green Capitalism: The God that failed.* World Economics Association (WEA), Book Series, Volume 5. College Publications (on behalf of WEA). Available at www.worldeconomicsassociation.org

Swedish Environmental Agency, 2016. *Environmental Objectives.* www.miljomal.se/sv/Environmental-Objectives-Portal/ (Accessed October 16, 2016)

Söderbaum, Peter, 2000. *Ecological Economics: A political economics approach to environment and development.* Earthscan, London.

Söderbaum, Peter and Judy Brown, 2010. Democratizing economics: Pluralism as a path toward sustainability. Annals of the New York Academy of Sciences 1185 *(Ecological Economics Reviews,* edited by Robert Costanza and Karin Limburg), pp. 179–195.

Söderbaum, Peter, 2013. Ecological economics in relation to democracy, ideology, and politics, Ecological Economics Vol. 95, pp. 221–225.

Söderbaum, Peter, 2015. Varieties of ecological economics: Do we need a more open and radical version of ecological economics? Ecological Economics Vol. 119, pp. 420–423.

Söderbaum, Peter, 2016. *Economics, ideological orientation, and democracy for sustainable development.* World Economics Association (WEA) e-Books. Available at www.worldeconomicsassociation.org.

Söderbaum, Peter, 2017. How Economics Can Become Compatible with Democracy, Chapter 2, pp. 25–38 in Stanislav Shmelev Ed. *Green Economy Reader: Lectures in Ecological Economics and Sustainability.* Springer International Publishing AG, Switzerland.

United Nations Sustainable Development Platform, 2016. http://www.un.org/sustainable development/sustainable-development-goals/ (Accessed 2016-10-14).

BIOMIMICRY:
THE VALUE OF ECOSYSTEM SERVICES

Jacques Chirazi

History shows that human well-being is strongly linked to the capacity of human environments to continue to deliver ecosystem services at the local to regional scale. The best-established example is Easter Island in the southeast Pacific. The Polynesian people settled the previously uninhabited island around 900 AD. They thrived initially, but eventually denuded the island of forest. The deforestation led to massive soil erosion, impairing the growth of staple crops and further reducing the resiliency of endemic species (fauna and flora). In consequence, from an estimated peak population of around 7,000 in the fifteenth century, numbers diminished, environmental and social conditions deteriorated, and warfare and cannibalism broke out. We need to learn these important lessons of history to help us develop a regenerative and resilient socioeconomic system based on systems thinking and sustainability to ensure future generations wellbeing and survival.

The essential ecological services that nature provides are primordial to human welfare and can't be replaced by other apparatus. Life support services like purification of air, photosynthesis, soil formation, biodiversity, oxygenation, carbon, nitrogen and hydrological cycles, and climate regulation can't be substituted, and without them, humans wouldn't be able to survive and thrive.

The valuation of these services is challenging to assess and measure, given that they are all interconnected and interdependent. Economists estimate the worth of the entire biosphere of ecological services to be in the range of $16–54 trillion per year (in comparison, the global gross national product is approx. $18 trillion per year).

Yet, because most of these benefits are not traded in economic markets, they carry no price tags that could alert society to changes in their supply or deterioration of underlying ecological systems that generate them. Because threats to these services are increasing, there is a critical need for the incorporation of their values into decision-making processes and embedding ecosystem services into corporate management systems.

Human ingenuity may develop replacement technologies (e.g., geoengineering for climate regulation, hand pollination) for some of these ecological service functions. However, these man-made solutions will have very high economic and social costs. Conservation, preservation, restoration, and regeneration of ecological services are more viable options and would lead to a resilient socioeconomic system.

According to the World Economic Forum's (WEF's) Global Risks 2014 report of the top ten risks deemed most likely and significant, four are economic, two societal, and four environmental.

Table 1: Ten Global Risks of Highest Concern in 2014

No.	GLOBAL RISK
1.	Fiscal crises in key economies
2.	Structurally high unemployment/underemployment
3.	Water crises
4.	Severe income disparity
5.	Failure of climate change mitigation and adaptation
6.	Higher incidence of extreme weather events (e.g., floods, storms, fires)
7.	Global governance failure
8.	Food crises
9.	Failure of a major financial mechanism/institution
10.	Profound political and social instability

Fiscal crisis is at the top, but water (ranked third), climate change (ranked fifth) and extreme weather events (ranked sixth) are all near the top of the list. The challenge for business and political leaders is therefore in how to build resilience into our economic, environmental and social systems at the same time.

Vis medicatrix naturae—this Latin term describes the concept of healing from nature. Our bodies have a profound capacity for self-repair and healing from within. So does nature, and we can act as healers. Humans have an opportunity to learn from nature's genius and apply this knowledge to our biggest challenges and to begin the restoration of our ecological services. This paradigm shift is essential to the survival of humanity. We need to re-learn how to become better stewards of the earth by reconnecting with nature and showing respect and humility to all life forms.

WHAT IS BIOMIMICRY?

Biomimicry is an approach to innovation that seeks sustainable solutions to human challenges by emulating nature's time-tested patterns and strategies. Nature can serve as a great model, measure, and mentor for the human species. Through more than 3.8 billion years of evolution, its organisms have adapted to earth's varied operating conditions with elegant and efficient strategies. These organisms are the consummate engineers and have already solved many of the problems we are grappling with: energy production and storage, water, food production, transportation, non-toxic chemistry, and more. Biomimicry technologies have led to new, more efficient methods of water harvesting and filtration, energy generation and distribution, and more. The goal of biomimicry is to create products, processes, systems, and policies that will help make life on earth more sustainable and valuable for future generations to come. The discipline of biomimicry is an underused opportunity to use lessons taken from nature to drive innovation and sustainability. It can guide startups and SMEs in creating disruptive innovation that can drive financial growth, raise valuation, lower costs, and spur untapped markets and industries.

To get a better sense of what biomimicry is, one must differentiate it from other bio-approaches like bio-utilization and bio-assistance. Bio-utilization is the harvesting of a natural product or the harnessing of a biological producer. Bio-assistance involves domesticating an organism to accomplish a function. Instead of using or growing organisms, biomimicry takes inspiration from nature's physical form, functional processes, or system principles. Another important distinction is the difference between well-adapted and maladapted practices. Well-adapted practices create conditions conducive to life, whereas maladapted practices may be unsustainable or unethical. If a biomimetic solution is harmful or manufactured and transported by energy-intensive and toxic processes, it misses the point of true biomimicry. The commercialization of biomimicry is not solely technical. It also requires an emerging business model that incorporates nature's adaptability and resiliency. Social entrepreneurship has emerged over the past few decades as an innovative business model to enable radical socioeconomic transformations and foster the next generation of sustainable entrepreneurs.

FORMULATING AN IDEA

There are two main methods of formulating a biomimicry idea: problem-driven and solution-driven. The problem-driven approach occurs when a party or company is seeking to solve a challenge (whether product, process, or system related) and looks to nature for solutions. This approach is most common wherever a gap exists or there is a need for improvement and R&D investment in new technology. As an example, Interface Corporation, a carpet manufacturer, looked to the forest in hopes of finding ways to make their product more sustainable and environmentally friendly. Taking inspiration from the forest floor, it created a modular carpet with random patterns and were able to reduce waste by enabling consumers to replace individual worn carpet tiles instead of entire carpeted floors, as is the case with traditional carpet colors and patterns. The company continued to use biomimicry to incorporate recycling and to detoxify their industrial process. Although a slower process, the problem-driven method can bring effective solutions to the table (and eventually to market).

The solution-driven approach occurs when inspiration takes root in biological phenomena and develops into a solution. In other words, an effective technology application inspired by nature is identified and pushed through R&D, manufacturing, and sales/marketing onto the market. Many well-known examples of biomimicry products and startup companies occupy this category. In the case of Sharklet Technologies, Dr. Tony Brennan discovered that sharks have a naturally anti-fouling skin. This surface comprises an arrangement of micropatterns (called denticles) which discourage microorganisms from colonizing it.

The company applied this new technology to create structure-based antibacterial products like catheters or sanitary surfaces.

Although learning from nature is not novel (Leonardo da Vinci's designs five centuries ago, Velcro inspired by burrs), it is not widely embraced in the modern market. This creates an opening for the development and deployment of breakthrough innovations which can go on to disrupt the market status quo. Often, biomimicry disruptive technologies may even create new market niches or alter existing ones. Emerging sustainability trends have pushed hard for markets like renewable energy, sustainable agriculture, green chemistry, and transportation. Never-before-seen design strategies in nature may also cause a paradigm shift in previously stagnant areas of science, technology, and commercialization. Before WhalePower, it was assumed that the leading edge of any aerodynamic foil, such as wings on a plane and blades on wind turbines or fans, should be smooth. However, Dr. Frank Fish took a closer look at the bumps on the leading edges of humpback whale flippers and found, much to his bewilderment, that this was not the case. This discovery, named Tubercle Technology, led to a new understanding of fluid dynamics that has overturned previous assumptions and provided new methods of improving performance.

These are all amazing examples of biomimicry solutions, but the path to commercialization is not straightforward. The ideal strategy to mimic in nature may not be obvious. With an estimated 10–30 million species on the planet and millions of biological processes, there are numerous models and functions from which to learn. Also, many biological strategies may not be well understood and often require extensive research to apply. The development of a commercial solution takes multiple iterations before a final design is in sight. These time commitments make for a slow commercialization process, as researchers and engineers, designers, and entrepreneurs work in conjunction to transform a nature-inspired idea into a commercially viable innovation.

To enable a paradigm shift in mindset, we must support the STEAM curriculum, based on the idea of educating students in five specific disciplines; science, technology, engineering, the arts, and mathematics—in an interdisciplinary and applied approach. Rather than teach the five disciplines as separate and standalone subjects, STEAM integrates them into a cohesive learning paradigm based on real-world applications. Collaborative and open innovation are essential drivers to a regenerative a resilient economy which can pioneer radical design ideas and spark broad socioeconomic and environmental benefits. Small and medium enterprises are the cornerstone of the economy and key actors in shifting our economy toward sustainable development and circular models.

BIOMIMICRY DESIGN PROCESS

The biomimicry design process has four main phases: scoping, discovering, creating, and evaluating. The scoping phase involves defining the problem/challenge, identifying what biological function is required to solve that problem, and trying to integrate life's principles (deep patterns found in nature) into the design. The discovery phase involves researching different models and biological strategies that provide novel approaches to problems that may arise. The creation phase involves moving from the abstract idea to a concrete product, process, and/or system, and finally, the evaluation phase involves measuring how the new product or process and/or system performs when compared to counterparts in nature and measured by life's principles. The biomimicry design process is not a set linear path; it can start in different phases depending on the task (problem-driven or solution driven) and often requires circling back.

A company may cycle through these design phases numerous times making several iterations of a product and innovative application. Sharklet Technology developed its first technology application for the marine and shipping industry. However, it later discovered, by coincidence, that its innovative design was not only effective in the marine and shipping industry but was even more well-suited to applications in the medical device industry. The medical device industry had an urgent need for perpetually sterile instruments, and Sharklet's technology provided this sterility disruptively. Sharklet has developed a series of products using this technology, but every time it does, the company takes this new approach back to the drawing board to restart the product development process.

Despite some set paths, there are still many aspects of innovation that require something extra to produce a viable product or solution. For many of the ideas that have resulted from the biomimicry design process, having a multidisciplinary team that can communicate and work together across disciplines is vital to turning the idea into a market-based solution. The team needs to understand the biological strategies and mechanisms, the translation of biology into engineering and design, market potential and viability and customer validation, to commercialize a successful biomimetic solution. It also needs a commitment to the design process that can transcend momentary setbacks. Using biomimetic ideas to come up with a design is a long, arduous process not necessarily filled with constant progress. Advancements often come in spurts with long periods of difficulties and stagnation in between.

Innovative design is important, but in order to develop the design and eventually move it to the market, obtaining funding is just as important. Since biomimicry is such a new design methodology, many entrepreneurs do not fully understand its potential or have not even heard of it. As a result, some investors may be reluctant to help fund biomimetic innovation, as they would rather invest in technologies that have already proven themselves in different markets. To overcome this obstacle, entrepreneurs in the biomimicry community have emphasized educating others about biomimicry thinking and its benefits. In addition to spreading the word about biomimicry to gain funding, grants from governments and other organizations are often of great value. In general, biomimicry provides deeper sustainable solutions to the human challenge, and this may attract governments or SME who value sustainability as well as market performance.

Biomimetic innovations are often novel, groundbreaking concepts that tend to go against conventional design thinking. Often, these disruptive innovations expand a market or even create their own. While this does mean that those who created the product will need to learn how to navigate a completely new market environment and identify what business model works in it, it also means they will face relatively meager competition in its early stages, especially in untapped markets.

INNOVATIVE STARTUPS & SMALL AND MEDIUM ENTERPRISES

Innovative startups and SMEs can become the engine of the sustainable economy and facilitate the transition to a resource efficient, climate-smart circular economy. They can play an important role in helping global economies move from a high-carbon to a low-carbon economy, engage in innovative approaches to ecosystem restoration, and spur job creation. The potential to commercialize innovative solutions from SMEs faces several barriers, including limited support for proof of concept development, limited risk financing, lack of prototyping support, and an insufficient or limited commercialization process. Growth, therefore, needs to be stimulated by increasing the levels of innovation in SMEs, covering their different needs over the whole innovation cycle and commercialization cycle. Innovative SMEs should be supported and guided to reach and accelerate their full sustainability growth potential.

Whether restoring a watershed to provide clean and reliable drinking water for a large urban community or restoring salt march for fisheries and storm protection, societies and governments can save billions of dollars by helping nature do what it does best. Investing in our ecological infrastructure is a cost-effective strategy for achieving national and global objectives, such as increased resilience to climate change, reduced risk from natural disaster, and improved food and water security—all of which directly alleviate poverty, build sustainable livelihoods, and create jobs.

A new economic approach that prioritizes investment in our ecological infrastructure is gaining increasing attention, giving real substance to that often vague and misleading phrase, the "Green Economy." A critical first step is the development of legislative and regulatory frameworks as well as innovative finance mechanisms and other incentives to protect and restore our natural capital. This new approach to investment must also consider appropriate scale and time horizons so that the values of, and trade-offs between, ecosystem services are used wisely to inform decision-making in both the public and private sectors.

EVOLUTION OF ENTREPRENEURSHIP AND SUSTAINABILITY

Fast forward to 2030, and many of the key trends we see around us will have come of age. According to UN predictions, we will be 9 billion people—60% living in urbanized areas—and 5 billion of us will be online, with the majority of the online community in Asia. For agile SMEs prepared to rethink traditional business models, this means real opportunities for business growth and the development of disruptive innovations.

Technology is also changing the ways people work and increasingly enabling machines and software to substitute for humans. Enterprises and individuals who can seize the opportunities offered by digital advances stand to gain significantly, while those who cannot may lose everything. The growth and prosperity of all economies, whether rapid-growth or maturity, remains highly dependent on entrepreneurial activity.

Entrepreneurs are the lifeblood of economic growth—they provide a source of income and employment for themselves, create jobs for others, produce new and innovative products or services, and drive greater upstream and downstream value-chain activities. While necessity still drives some entrepreneurial activity around the world, "high-impact" entrepreneurship, once mainly confined to mature markets, is now an essential driver of economic expansion in rapid-growth markets. In some cases, these high-impact entrepreneurs are building innovative and scalable enterprises that capitalize on local needs and serve as role models for new entrepreneurs. The face of entrepreneurship is also changing—across the world, entrepreneurs are increasingly young and/or female. Many of these new enterprises are digital from birth. Access to funding remains the primary obstacle for entrepreneurs from all markets. The public and private sector each have an important role in creating entrepreneurial ecosystems that, in addition to funding, are essential to promoting entrepreneurial success

Cities are economic engines. According to McKinsey, 600 cities are responsible for 60% of global GDP. The healthy economy of a city sustains its population through salaries and entrepreneurial activity. However, all economic activity is subject to disruption; shifts in business models can create new opportunities, but cities from Detroit to Liverpool have seen the possible downsides of industrial change.

By 2050, seven out of every ten people on Earth will be living in an urban environment. What the cities of the future will look like depends largely on decisions we make today.

Our cities are built brick by brick, often using construction practices that have evolved little in the last century and giving little regard to proper planning and sustainable development. Yet innovations and technologies have produced progressive means of constructing the built environment to ensure that urban infrastructure, once in place, can make a valuable contribution to the workings of a city for centuries to come, withstanding many changes in use and function. Good urban infrastructure needs to anticipate change, adapt and be resilient.

In the fourth industrial revolution, we are likely to see the biggest industrial shifts in a generation, changing the way we work and live in the urban environment. Innovations such as nanotechnologies, personal medicine, 3D-printing, artificial intelligence, machine learning and next-generation robotics will shift models of work and production in ways that are impossible to predict. Cities and businesses need to be adaptive. Google, a company at the forefront of this change, anticipates that its business model could shift dramatically. Its new Mountain View headquarters is adapted for this: it is a series of giant domes under which it can quickly assemble any number of structures, fit for any purpose, making them completely reprogrammable for any eventual use case. Cities need to take a similar approach to construction.

The sharing economy can be defined as the distribution and sharing of excess goods and services between individuals, largely enabled by modern technology. This new model is having a deep impact on the urban environment. Many consumers are moving away from ownership and toward access, renting access to mobility, entertainment, or space.

Humanity faces the mammoth task of adding over 2 billion people to the urban population before 2050, the equivalent of creating a city the size of London every month for the next two decades. To house, feed, and employ these people, cities will have to do more with less: they will have to be smarter, greener and more efficient. They will have to innovate.

CONCLUSION

Natural processes have been a source of creative inspiration for human innovators for thousands of years. For most of this time, however, the technology, knowledge base, and intellectual property protections available to innovators has been insufficient, limiting both the complexity and the profitability of biomimetic inventions. More importantly, while nature may have circumstantially inspired individual innovators, there was no clearly defined innovation and commercialization process to follow: very often, innovation was the result of a fortuitous accident. Even more often, the innovator would not be compensated for his work.

Over the last few decades, however, this state of affairs has changed dramatically. Today, dozens of start-ups and established companies are leveraging natural structures and processes to carve out a premium niche for themselves in a competitive market or to directly create a completely new market in which they have undisputed power. The process of designing, proving, and finally commercializing any product—including nature-inspired biomimetic products—is very challenging. However, as we have seen in previously described examples, when done right, biomimicry has the potential to disrupt entire industries and sectors.

Nature is a sustainable system, and therefore solutions inspired by natural processes are more durable and efficient than their traditional design. Being environmentally responsible is always a reward unto itself, but in this case, sustainability is lucrative: it is possible to achieve higher profits by making a small contribution to the salvation of our planet.

In closing: biomimicry is making a tangible difference in the bottom lines of a great many firms today. Biomimetic innovation and design, when done right, offers startups and SMEs an unparalleled opportunity to make the world a better place while increasing profitability instead of reducing it. Finally, if ecological services were the basis of money, then instead of going toward production and consumption of goods and services, it would go toward conservation and restoration of ecological systems. This is the pathway that leads to sustainability for humanity and our planet. We need to radically rethink our economic, financial, political, and social systems to begin this journey toward a truly sustainable world that would provide long-term prosperity for future generations.

COMMUNITY-BASED ECONOMIC DEVELOPMENT:
LEARNING FROM EMPLOYEE OWNERSHIP AND SOCIAL ENTERPRISE

Darcy Hitchcock

Adapted from *Great Work: 12 Principles for Your Work Life and Life's Work* by Darcy Hitchcock

THE LINE BETWEEN FOR-PROFITS AND NONPROFITS IS GETTING FUZZY

Historically, businesses make money, governments provide a safety net, and charities take up the slack. But as expectations of business have ramped up, including the expectations of millennials, new organizational forms are emerging, blurring the lines between business and nonprofits.

Like many organizations working to provide skills, training, and experience, the International Society of Sustainability Professionals (ISSP) seeks to make sustainability standard practice. What does this mean? For ISSP, it means empowering individuals and professionals to advance sustainability in organizations and communities throughout the globe. These organizations include traditional businesses, social enterprises, and nonprofits. The goal of this organization and many others is to expand thinking about the myriad of possibilities in promoting community development, welfare, and work.

One such possibility is community-based economic development (CBED). Offering an alternative to current left-brain oriented business-as-usual, CBED proposes first identifying local community needs, identifying local businesses which could organize to serve those needs, bringing together residents who could help fund (in money or in kind) the effort, employing local people who need work, in a cooperative model in which workers reap the majority of the wealth. I developed this concept based on my observations of social enterprises, NGOs, certified B corporations, and employee ownership models.

Social enterprise spans the space between pure nonprofits and traditional corporations. They expressly intend to make a social (or environmental) difference in the world, employing markets as a business would. These span a huge range of industries, from education to economic development, medicine to manufacturing. Famous examples include the Grameen Bank in India with its microloans and Kiva.org, a US-based platform that allows individuals to lend small amounts interest-free to people around the world.

Some NGOs (nonprofits) have responded by creating for-profit businesses where the profits go toward charities. For example, the late actor Paul Newman created a food company, and 100 percent of the profits go to the Newman's Own Foundation. From selling salad dressings, the company has expanded into different food items, including pet food. By 2012, the foundation had given grants of over $350 million to charities around the world, arguably much more than if it had stayed with a pure nonprofit model.

Greyston Bakery in Yonkers, New York, is a more complicated picture. The bakery was created to provide jobs to people who needed them. They hire whoever shows up on a first-come basis. The profits from the bakery go to their foundation, which then in turn funds more social programs.

Because the for-profit operation is also providing an important social benefit, Greyston became certified as a B Corp, a for-benefit corporation giving documentation proving its social and environmental benefit. This helps differentiate B Corporations from other similar businesses, and some states have written into their purchasing guidelines that they can give preference to B Corps. B Lab, the certifying body, started in the United States but has now spread to 50 countries. Every two years, B Corps are audited and recertified.

C. K. Prahalad's book *Fortune at the Bottom of the Pyramid* gave us the term "bottom of the pyramid," though some have renamed it the "base" of the pyramid to be less offensive (BoP). Whatever one calls it, many of the largest consumer companies are experimenting with repackaging their products for the poorest of the poor. In *Capitalism at the Crossroads,* author Stuart Hart indicates that this may be the only remaining large market opportunity for companies that have saturated the developed world.

While it may seem immoral for rich corporations to sell products to the poorest of the BoP, the uncomfortable truth is that many poor people have to pay *more for services than those with greater incomes. The wealthier can buy in bulk, such as a liter bottle of clothes detergent, while the poor may be only able to afford a single-use packet.* Those with adequate income purchase cheap electricity from a utility but the BoP may pay many times that in kerosene. Credit card interest rates may chafe, but they are puny compared to loan sharks charging 25 percent a month! Agree with him or not, Stuart Hart, author of *Capitalism at the Crossroads,* believes:

> *Business—more than either government or civil society—is uniquely equipped at this point in history to lead us toward a sustainable world in the years ahead. Corporations are the only entities in the world today with the technology, resources, capacity and global reach required. Properly focused, the profit motive can accelerate (not inhibit) the transformation toward global sustainability, with nonprofits, governments, and multilateral agencies all playing crucial roles as collaborators and watchdogs.*
>
> —Fortune at the Bottom of the Pyramid

What's interesting is that *lack* of money is a powerful force for innovation:

- Jaipur Foot designed a prosthesis for rural areas, allowing necessary movement such as squatting and walking on uneven ground. The Jaipur foot sells for about $30, compared to products in the US costing $8,000. They have held camps in twenty-six countries, helping those who lose limbs from landmines and other accidents or genetic deformities.
- Aravind Eye Care performs 95,000 world-class eye surgeries a year in India. The surgeries, which cost approximately $3,000 in the US, cost only $50–300, and 60% of patients get the surgery for free! Paying patients subsidize those who cannot pay. Because Avarind couldn't afford intraocular lenses sold by other manufacturers for $200 each, they invented a process to make them for a few dollars. The quality of care is so good that the United Kingdom started sending patients to India for surgery to save on healthcare costs.

COOPERATIVES MAKE A DIFFERENCE TO EMPLOYEES

Many people think of cooperatives as food stores where the customers are part owners. But they include agricultural co-ops of farmers or dairies, where suppliers are the owners. The worker-owned co-op, for example, can spread power and wealth more equitably through the organization.

In 2014, the *Harvard Business Review* included an article called, "CEOs get paid too much, according to pretty much everyone in the world." Gretchen Gavett puts the pay gap into historical perspective:

We're currently far past the late Peter Drucker's warning that any CEO-to-worker ratio larger than 20:1 would "increase employee resentment and decrease morale." Twenty years ago it had already hit 40 to 1, and it was around 400 to 1 at the time of his death in 2005 . . . it's mind-bogglingly difficult for ordinary people to even guess at the actual differences between the top and the bottom.

In her research, Gavett discovered that most felt CEOs should get about 4.6 to 1 as compared to unskilled workers. With technology replacing jobs and globalization undermining union wages, the gap is exacerbated and is becoming a source of social unrest. While some companies like Ben and Jerry's ice cream company have tried to institute a pay cap for executives, in practice these often get snuffed out by stockholders and boards who feel it makes it too difficult to attract top talent.

One elegant solution is the worker-owned cooperative, where the workers *are* the owners. This form of ownership is often overlooked by attorneys who help entrepreneurs set up their businesses and by the media, even though they can be highly successful businesses where employees benefit directly from the wealth they create.

Mondragon in Spain spans a wide range of businesses. In 2010 it generated just under 14 billion euros in sales and employed about 100,000 people. It operates democratically, emphasizing self-management. It invests about 10 percent of its profits in social activities ranging from research and education to cultural activities and social support services. Mondragon is committed to maintaining employment rather than profit margins, so if one business is struggling, employees get retrained and loaned to others. This meant that in 2008, while many in the United States and much of the world were thrown out of work by the Great Recession, Mondragon quickly transferred laid-off employees to other companies within Mondragon. By 2010, most were back at their regular jobs again.

Some claim Mondragon's success was due to its homogeneous culture and socialistic leanings. But cooperatives have been successful in many different settings, sometimes even started by youth.

Mountain Equipment Cooperative (MEC) was started by six students in 1971 in Canada with just C$65 of operating capital to provide outdoor equipment with a low markup on the gear offered and operated with democratic principles. Forty years later, three million people in Canada and around the world share the original philosophy and are members of the cooperative which has annual sales of C$261 million. Widely recognized for its commitment to sustainability, MEC is Canada's leading outdoor retailer.

The Evergreen Cooperatives in Cleveland were inspired by Mondragon. At one time, the inner city had become hollowed out by poverty and racial unrest. But there were several keystone institutions—the Cleveland Clinic, University Hospitals, Case Western Reserve University—cordoned-off oases with employees driving past people in miserable conditions, who would park and dash inside their place of business. These and a few other local institutions bought over $3 billion in goods and services. They realized that by pooling their purchasing power, they could launch businesses—employee-owned cooperatives—that could employ people from the surrounding low-income neighborhoods, providing services they needed at a lower carbon footprint, buying local with a twist. The first was a laundry. Some of the employees used to be in prison or deal drugs. Now they are responsible workers and supervisors. After six months, an employee begins to contribute to an ownership fund. In a community where people lucky enough to have jobs only earn about $18,000 in median income, these worker-owners are projected in eight years to have $65,000 each in equity in their business.

Cooperatives are a more fair way to allocate wealth than business as usual. Rather than having the lion's share go to the CEO or people who only bought stock with a click of a button, why not have most of it go to all the people who work hard forty or more hours a week to make it thrive?

WHY NOT A BIT OF BOTH?

As we look to the future, the real opportunity is to blend social enterprise with worker-owned and democratically-run cooperatives. Devise a venture that will do good in the world and at the same time, choose an organizational form to empower and enrich the employees.

Examples are hard to find, but here is one that exemplifies what can be done.

Cooperative Home Care Associates in New York has a staff of 2,300 owners, mostly poor, minority women who were unemployed. It provides home care for elderly or disabled Medicaid patients at home. In addition to being owners in the business, its workers get time-and-a-half for overtime, extremely rare in the industry.

This gap between enterprises that are created to help society versus enterprises created to empower workers suggests a closer look at the traditional approach to economic development. Usually, this involves luring large firms from elsewhere with generous tax breaks to provide jobs the local people usually don't have. Recently Tesla received a $1 billion tax deal to site its battery plant in Nevada.

Some wonder whether the big tax breaks it took to land the deal are worth the larger costs to the state. Among the estimated 240 tax subsidies worth more than $75 million passed by state legislatures since 1976, the average has cost a state $456,000 per job, according to the Good Jobs First report.

COMMUNITY-BASED ECONOMIC DEVELOPMENT

What happens when we put these ideas into public policy, as an economic development strategy? Traditionally, economic development has often sought outside companies to bring into the community. The thinking is that large corporations can bring in a lot of new jobs, so it's worth offering lots of tax credits to bring them into town. There are, however, obvious shortcomings of putting all economic development efforts into this approach:

- Companies with fewer than twenty employees add the most jobs, and large firms are shedding jobs.
- When companies *move* to one location from somewhere else, they can devastate the community they are leaving—a zero-sum game.
- Non-local, often subsidized enterprises are more likely to pick up and leave since the investors aren't grounded in the community.
- The tax breaks undermine one of the main purposes of economic growth: to bolster tax revenues to provide local services.
- Non-local companies often focus on the export market, which can lead to higher greenhouse gas emissions and various social impacts.
- Because these enterprises often have home bases elsewhere, capital leaves the community faster.
- The organizations tend to be shareholder-driven rather than stakeholder-driven, so the wealth created tends not to go to the people doing the work but rather gets concentrated in the hands of a few, making an inequitable society even more so.
- It sets up the need for workforce development training, which still leaves a large percentage of the population behind.

> **We live in capitalism. Its power seems inescapable.
> So did the divine right of kings.
> Any human power can be resisted and changed by human beings.**
>
> —Ursula K. Le Guin, sci-fi author

So what is an alternative? I propose a concept I call community-based economic development (CBED). Just imagine if we first identified local community needs which local businesses could then organize to serve and which, if needed, residents could help fund so they could employ local people who need jobs in a cooperative model, so the workers get the lion's share of the wealth. This changes the questions we should be asking.

Question 1. What Does the Community Need?

Traditional economic development doesn't care much about what jobs it creates or what the business does; it just wants more jobs. But CBED asks that we start with the question: What does the community need? If startup funding was necessary, don't go to the *Shark Tank* TV show (where high-rolling investors take a huge chunk of stock ownership in exchange for startup capital); create a system that allows *local* people to invest. If those businesses are appropriate to be employee-owned cooperatives, then the economic engine really starts to crank!

Question 2. Who Needs Opportunities?

After identifying the need, identify who might be interested in solving this problem who also needs an opportunity to work. At this point, still recovering from the Great Recession of 2008 and the aging demographics of most developed countries, we don't just have the traditionally hard-to-employ population. We also have laid-off baby boomers (people born shortly after World War II) who will likely never get another traditional job. And we have entrepreneurial young people coming out of school filled with idealism and disinclined to climb someone else's ladder. These three groups have synergistic qualities which can make for better work opportunities for the youth of the future.

What if, once we identified a community need, we gathered up people from all three of these groups (laid-off boomers, young adults and those who are struggling) to work together to create their own opportunities?

Stop waiting for someone else to create a job for you. Make your own!

Question 3. What Are Examples of Community Needs and Associated Business Opportunities?

As mentioned earlier, Cooperative Home Care Associates takes care of the elderly and disabled in their homes. But here are other ideas that only require basic skills that many of the unemployed might have:

- After-school programs for kids. In the United States, many people complain about the loss of music, art, and athletic programs. Why not offer after-school programs to fill in the gap?
- Food carts which can take food or groceries to shut-ins or so-called food-deserts where residents don't have easy access to fresh produce and healthy eating.
- Installing energy/water conservation gizmos or solar panels in lower-income housing.
- Gathering edible but wasted food from restaurants and groceries and use it to feed the hungry.

Here are some that are even appropriate for immigrants who haven't yet mastered the local language:

- Language training—Teaching travelers or tutor students trying to learn a foreign language
- Making pre-prepared healthy meals for families too busy to cook every night
- Cooking classes—Teaching their local cuisine and produce
- Housecleaning and household repair services for the elderly living alone
- Farming—Growing produce for a local farmers market

These business ideas aren't likely to land an organization on a Wall Street stock exchange (and thank heaven for that, since becoming a public corporation is a great way to lose control over your life). Some would even work fine as part-time employment for people going to school to get off state welfare or parents with young children. But that's okay. If we can create opportunities (note I didn't say "jobs") for people to supplement their income, gain work experience, and solve their own community or personal problems at the same time, why not do it? An extra $5,000 or $10,000 in a poor person's pocket can make a huge difference in their lives. Of course, nothing is stopping you from creating an enterprise requiring higher skills.

- Nurses and physician assistants could offer house calls.
- Professionals could offer to tutor or mentor at-risk youth.
- Building professionals could create a firm focusing on green building for low-income housing.

Question 4. So What's Needed to Make CBED Work?

There are challenges to this model in the current economy. This concept of community-based economic development is still an untested idea; pieces are in place here and there but not as a coherent strategy. Here are some questions you might ponder if you want to pursue this alternative to traditional economic development:

- How do we get information about community needs better, faster, cheaper? Funding is weak for community assessments. Can we leverage crowdsourcing, smartphones, and the like to do rapid market research or poll for priorities? What if high school kids had an app that turned them into pollsters as they went around town? When prompted, could they ask someone near them about community needs? Perhaps methods like participatory budgeting (where citizens vote on ideas to fund) can engage a community that is struggling.
- How do we redirect much of the capital that is going to the old economy to a community-based strategy? Communities are experimenting with local investment systems, redirecting money from Wall Street to Main Street. Check out the approaches by James Frazier, founder of Local Investment Opportunities Network (LION) and Local Investing Resources Center, and Renata B. Kowalczyk, co-founder of Whatcom Investing Network. Some people have completely reworked their retirement accounts around loans to local businesses.
- How do we help people make their own opportunities using skills they already have? Imagine immigrant populations developing community gardens to grow special produce unique to their traditions. We could aid them in this and then set them up with food carts so they could sell to locals, outside offices, and serve as Meals on Wheels to shut-ins in their community.
- How can we find and combine people from these three populations (traditionally unemployed, boomers, and young people) into viable social enterprises? We need to stop trying to "fix" them in silos. Connect them! How do we help people who may feel disempowered to be more entrepreneurial?
- What other systems need to be in place? Do we need more business incubators with experience in employee-owned

cooperatives? What needs to be done to bolster the informal economy? Would time banks or alternative currencies provide a medium of exchange for people without much money?

Community-based economic development is still just a concept that pulls together a variety of trends, including a focus on local purchasing, an interest in cooperatives, the millennials' tendency to cobble together a living, and a desire to grow jobs from within a community rather than finding a white knight.

LOOKING TO THE FUTURE: TIPS FOR CHOOSING THE BEST ORGANIZATIONAL FORM

Pure nonprofits work directly on issues but then can struggle to get enough funding to scale up solutions. For-profit businesses may or may not see their role in creating a more just and sustainable world, and large corporations can be hard to change. For many, the fun opportunities are somewhere in between those two poles.

If you are choosing between the power of a democratic workplace or the security of ownership, my advice is to choose the power.

For example, the mid-level manager may not be in a position to reform the organization. However, they may be able to model the benefits of a cooperative by using empowering practices and changing the compensation system to gainsharing, so that a significant portion of the organization's or team's profits goes to employees.

Don't confuse ownership with empowerment, and don't do ownership without empowerment. Major academic studies show that companies with ESOPs, employee stock ownership plans, grow in sales, employment, and productivity faster than would have been predicted without an ESOP. ESOPs are associated with higher returns on assets and stock prices. In successful ESOPs, companies combine ownership with an "ownership culture," giving employees influence on day-to-day decisions and regularly sharing detailed corporate performance data.

In 1995, United Airlines created an ESOP. I warned the airline's human resources director that it would fail if they didn't develop participative structures. After five years, the ESOP was dead. The National Center for Employee Ownership found that while the ESOP did not cause United to fail, it "abjectly" failed to help the company the way most ESOPs do. United's unions used the ESOP to prevent United from breaking up into regional carriers, diversifying out of the airline business, and outsourcing work performed by union members. They succeeded. Management saw the ESOP primarily as a way to get wage concessions. They succeeded in their goal as well.

If you are unemployed and having trouble finding a job, consider creating your own. Explore the CBED strategy. What community problem would you love to solve? Who else could help you? Is there training, support, and funding available to help you get started?

Entrepreneurs should think long and hard about the legacy they want to leave. Do they just want to get rich or do they want to build wealth in the community? Ideally, they create organizational forms that support social and environmental justice while also providing real power and wealth to all who do the work.

ABOUT THE AUTHOR

Darcy Hitchcock has a knack for translating the theory of sustainability into practical and actionable tools. She is the author of the award-winning *The Business Guide to Sustainability* (now in its third edition), *The Step by Step Guide to Sustainability Planning*, an educational novella called *Dragonfly's Question*, and more recently, *Great Work: 12 Principles for Your Work Life and Life's Work*. She spent over fifteen years as a sustainability consultant and co-founded the International Society of Sustainability Professionals. Darcy recently retired from her sustainability consulting practice and is now living in Sedona. She likes to say she's still working for change, just not often for money. She founded the Sustainability Alliance, a coalition of nonprofits, where they are, among other projects, launching a business certification and easing sustainability practices into schools. For more information, go to www.SustainabilityAllianceAZ.org or DarcyHitchcock.wordpress.com.

CONTRIBUTING TO A CULTURE OF MULTIGENERATIONAL UNITY: LEADERSHIP TO CONNECT IN EXTRAORDINARILY "SEMI-PERFECT" WAYS

Carolin Rekar Munro

One of the preeminent challenges which organizations grapple with today, and likely will face in the future, is bridging generational differences in the workplace. With five generations working alongside each other, we have witnessed not only a unique synergy of gifts and talents but also a surge in workplace conflicts. These conflicts, stemming from generational differences in attitudes, priorities, expectations, and work styles, are pervasive, persistent, and polarizing. They permeate all aspects of organizational life, from informal exchanges in the hallway to formal discourse in the boardroom, and they chip away at relationships with others, affecting how we listen to and respond to each other. If left unattended, these conflicts seep into the bloodstream of an organization's culture and stain the sacred grounds of productivity, profitability, employee and customer satisfaction, and employee turnover. Consequently, the sustainability and prosperity of our organizations are at risk. Without a shift in how multiple generations work together, this downward spiral likely will persist.

This essay is a call to action *for you*—the newest generation entering the workforce in the next decade. Its purpose is twofold: 1) to share with you the multigenerational landscape which will be your workplace reality; and, 2) to encourage and guide you to lead in contributing to a culture of multigenerational collaboration and inclusivity. Offered are tools for you to navigate the richness and complexity of communication in a multigenerational workplace. In doing so, it is anticipated you will see yourself as a partner in building and sustaining strong and long-term relationships in the workplace.

You might be curious as to why the title of this essay refers to *semi*-perfection. In reality, it is impossible to achieve *perfection*, especially as it pertains to human relationships. By seeking *semi*-perfect connection, we set our sights more realistically on being *the best we can be*. We'll aim for the best, realizing we won't always be in perfect sync with others. Occasionally, we might strike the wrong cord and cause conversations to go awry. Be willing to learn from this and keep building your capacity for stronger workplace relationships.

THE WORKPLACE OF THE FUTURE

Waiting for you in the labor market is a vibrant playground of opportunities with five inimitable generations—traditionalists, baby boomers, Generation X, Generation Y, and Generation Z. Before proceeding into an exploration of each generation, it is important to be mindful that the following descriptions are not intended to label generations with one sweeping brushstroke. In reality, not every member of a generation falls exactly within the parameters of the portrait—some less so than others. The purpose of the descriptions is to showcase the overarching characteristics of each generation; specifically, how they experience and perceive the world. These descriptions are not meant to be exhaustive characterizations. They are intended to provide a few differentiators which give us common understanding and language for our dialogue about ways to unify the generations.

The latest generation in the cue for full-time entry into the labor market is *you*—Generation Z (Gen Z). Born after 1995, your cohort wears the title of being the first truly mobile-first generation (Renfrow, 2012); that is, you are the most digitally connected generation in history, with exposure to media consuming the majority of your time, second only to sleep (Rideout et al., 2010). You are capable of sifting through enormous amounts of information with ease and, you rely almost exclusively on trending pages within apps as your source of information. You hold information received from others as highly suspect until it can be verified online (Good, et al., 2015). More than previous generations, you are likely to evolve into electronic multitaskers, even before you begin school (Renfrow, 2012). Other generations refer to you as screen addicts and raise concerns that technology may inhibit your ability to connect socially and in person (Toronto, 2009).

Raised in a world where war and terrorism are prevalent, your generation tends to view the world as unsafe. However, this cognizance of world events has contributed to your extensive global awareness, which is greater than that of other generations (Tulgan, 2012). As well, it has shaped your fiscal responsibility, your diversity-consciousness, and your advocacy for equality (Palley, 2012). However, it has also contributed to a high level of corporate distrust within your cohort (Montana & Petit, 2008). Other Gen Z identifiers include: drive to pursue higher education with the expectation of securing your dream job within ten years of graduation, inclination to job jump more than other generations; preference for self-education rather than allowing others to control what, how, and when you learn; and commitment to personal brand building (Hulyk, 2015).

Your close cousins in the generational mix are Generation Y (Gen Y), born 1981–2000. A decade from now, when the majority of our current workplace leaders retire, Gen Y will hold the leadership reins. Like yourselves, Gen Y has grown up thriving on the frenzied speed of technology, and they are known for job-jumping when frustrated with lack of, or denied, promotional opportunities (Beeson, 2009). Attributes which differentiate Gen Y from your generation include the following: more assertiveness in declaring their needs and expectations (Howe & Strauss, 2000); distinction as the highest performing, most ambitious, and hardest-working to get recognition for their leadership capabilities (Gilburg, 2008); and the most entrepreneurial generation in history (Martin, 2005). They are the most exigent generation for organizations to attract and retain because self-employment has greater appeal to them than working for a corporation (Lipkin & Perrymore, 2009). They are referred to as trophy kids: those who never lost anything, but received everything and are rewarded more often for effort than achievement (Alsop, 2013). Having fewer siblings, they are less experienced dealing with rivalry and competition (Strutton et al., 2011). From the workplace, they expect continuous recognition and instant feedback (Berkowitz & Schewe, 2011) and a climate rich with socializing and fun (Lamm & Meek, 2009). Gen Ys are often referred to as entitled, but they are quick to remind us that the entitlement we perceive is actually confidence, resulting from being raised by parents who instilled in them a determination to pursue their dreams and to be persistent and precise in declaring their wants and needs (Howe & Strauss, 2000).

The smallest cohort in most workplaces is Generation X (Gen X), born 1965–1980. They were the first generation to experience both parents entering the workplace; and, consequently, they spent a considerable amount of time alone focused primarily on video games and television (Lyons et al., 2007). As a result, they are more independent and self-reliant than other generations, reflected in their preference for work projects which require solo effort rather than collaboration and consultation (Barford & Hester, 2011). As well, Gen X is more skeptical and cynical about corporations, unimpressed by authority, and less inclined to pursue senior leadership positions (Crumpacker & Crumpacker, 2007). This came about as a result of witnessing massive organizational downsizing in which their parents lost their jobs after years of dedicated service. Gen X questioned the justice and fairness of this (Glass, 2007). There is a stark contrast between Gen X, which is known for its quiet patience in waiting for retirements to open doors for their promotion, and Gen Y, which is generally more assertive in declaring it needs and expecting promotion without waiting in the cue (Gursoy et al., 2008).

Baby boomers, born 1946–1964, take the prize for being the largest contingent in the workplace. By the time you are in the workplace, baby boomers will have retired or will be nearing retirement; however, you will see many of them returning to the workplace as consultants or in part-time jobs. Baby boomers were shaped by events such as the Vietnam War and the Civil Rights Movement, which instilled in them unwavering tenacity and persistence to collectively champion causes and rally for change (Burmeister, 2008). In the workplace, they pioneered diversity awareness and management programs; established comprehensive legislation protecting race, gender and people with disabilities; introduced metrification to calculate the return on investment of initiatives, and promoted degrees and professional designations as necessities for career advancement (Artley & Macon, 2009). Alongside these workplace contributions, they are known for core values of loyalty, optimism, justice and equality; a propensity to challenge authority; and preference for in-person communication (Martin & Tulgan, 2002). They are notorious for workaholism because of their steadfast loyalty to their organizations, drive to exceed expectations, and their view of work as that which defines you (Strauss & Howe, 1991).

Employees who have the longest standing seniority in our organizations are Traditionalists, born 1922–1945. By the time you are entrenched in the workplace, most Traditionalists will no longer be with us in our everyday work lives. However, they likely will maintain a powerful leadership presence on executive boards and advisory committees. This cohort weathered the Great Depression, and many of them are veterans of the military. As a result, they have a more directive approach to leadership; value working hard as an obligation, before having fun; view conformity, discipline, and compliance as non-negotiables; have a linear approach to problem-solving and decision making, prefer structure and formality in communication; and respect authority and the social order (Zemke et al., 2000). Traditionalists, credited with creating existing organizational structures and bureaucracies, are unwavering in their belief that the system was built right and built to last; hence, there is no need to question or change the workplace.

From the profiles of each generation, it is evident that work expectations, attitudes, and styles are entrenched deeply in the psyche of each, and these differences show up in how we act and react in the presence of others. Even though we might be tempted to point fingers at other generations and accuse them of being the culprits in our communication debacle, there is little value in doing this. Casting blame on others does not move us closer to getting our conversations and workplace connections back on track, and it implies that culpability for derailed engagement rests with others. If we are completely honest, we would admit that we all shoulder the responsibility. All generations have a significant role to play in bridging generational differences in the workplace.

COURAGEOUSLY EXERCISING YOUR LEADERSHIP

As the newest entrants in the workforce, you are invited to exercise your leadership to contribute to a culture of multigenerational unity. You are not expected to do all the heavy lifting, but you are encouraged to take the lead and model the way.

Even though you might be a tad hesitant about accepting the invitation, you are ideally suited for this role. You may not have the years of experience toiling in the workplace trenches, but this is, in reality, your signature strength. You come into the workplace looking at interactions between the generations through a refreshingly new lens and with curiosity about *why we do what we do*. From this unique vantage point, you often see what others have been missing. For example, other generations may have become set in their patterns of engagement and are not cognizant of how others perceive them; and, if they are aware, they may not know the pathway to better engagement. You can shed light on what others are not hearing, seeing, or doing; hence, you can be a catalyst for change. We anticipate that through modeling, your generation and later ones will follow suit and exercise their leadership to engage in new ways.

It is important to be mindful that, in the domain of human interactions, change happens incrementally over time. Change of this magnitude is not a sudden burst of 180-degree transformation in how we value, respect, and appreciate others. It won't be easy, and it promises to get messy before you find your footing. Success in closing the generational divide is incumbent on equipping ourselves with new tools to chisel forward; taking risks and risking mistakes until something sticks; listening deeply to advice from workplace veterans along the way; and respecting yourself and others, no matter how other people act and react and no matter what unexpectedly flies at you and challenges your patience.

Given the complexity of communication, it is unrealistic to assume an exhaustive set of tools can be provided. This essay will offer three that speak to the heart of workplace connectivity and provide you with a starting point for exercising your leadership in shaping engagement in our multigenerational workplaces.

GETTING OUT OF YOUR OWN WAY

At first glance, this appears to be a bizarre place to begin, yet it is an imperative step to take en route to forging workplace connectivity. You start by answering a critical and profound question: *How do I show up in the presence of others?* Specifically, do you let others see the authentic side of you, with its juxtaposition of strength and weakness, confidence and insecurity, and composure and fear?

Some of you might be thinking it is career suicide to show one's true self in the workplace. In actuality, it is the opposite. Expression of authenticity is vital to your ability to connect with others, influence them, and contribute to building a community of engagement and inclusivity. Revealing who you truly are, what you value, and why you do what you do is the magnet which compels people not only to want to be in your presence but to rally with and behind you, especially as you take on the important role of introducing new communication pathways. The more you reveal about yourself, the more people want to be in your presence because they realize they share more in common with you than they ever thought imaginable. This is a landmark realization in a work world where we perceive more differences than similarities between the generations.

What exactly do you need to start doing to become more authentic? Let go of who you think you are supposed to be; that is, free yourself from the behaviors which keep you from being your authentic self and keep others at bay. These could be the words you use to express yourself, your tone of voice, or your actions and reactions which signal you might not be approachable and others should keep their distance. Often a trusted confidante can coach you on this journey by providing feedback to guide you in charting one incremental step to be taken to reveal more of yourself to others.

If at any point, you show up *perfectly imperfect* and make a mistake, don't shy away from it. The worst things you can do are ignore it, make excuses, or blame others. By not owning up to the mistake, you likely will lose the respect of others. It is a long and arduous road to earning people's respect, but it doesn't take much to lose it. In reality, people around you care less about the mistake you made, and more about how you respond after it is exposed. Do you take ownership of it as soon as it is brought to your attention? Do you convey genuine remorse for what you did and communicate your understanding of the damage done?

Do you offer a concrete pathway for how you will rectify the situation? How you recover from the mistake is the focal point of their attention.

LEARNING A NEW LANGUAGE: FROM CRUSHERS TO CONNECTORS

Cognizance of our internal dialogue is one of the primary determinants of whether connections with others will be arms-length transactions or meaningful alliances. Our inner voice, with its intricately woven web of values, beliefs, attitudes, and assumptions, shapes not only our thinking but also our speech and our behaviors. For the most part, we don't realize the domino effect our private thoughts have on how we act and react to others, and how others experience us in conversation. Awareness of the power of our internal dialogue helps us explain why some conversations with others disintegrate in front of us and how we can turn the situation around.

When we show up with a predominantly evaluative presence, we can become a *conversation crusher*. We play the role of a critic who weighs in with judgment and criticism about the world around us. When evaluative people come together, the conversation tends to divide and disengage them because, for the most part, they focus on finding fault, refuting the beliefs of others, and seizing center stage to showcase their expert knowledge instead of leaving space for others to contribute.

Evaluation *can* play a salient role, but only in moderation. Reserve it for occasions when it makes a constructive and critical contribution to organizational or personal change: for example, when an expert critique of a workplace policy or practice is required or when assessment of performance is expected. The evaluation that has the potential to be a conversation crusher is that which does not add value. It is simply commentary for the sake of voicing one's opinion, and it does more harm than good.

When we show up with an inquisitive presence, we are on target to become a *conversation connector*. We enter into dialogue with an inexhaustible curiosity about the world, and we strive to comprehend and appreciate others, regardless of how divergent their beliefs and values are from our own. Conversation connecting takes the form of:

- asking more questions instead of having all the right answers
- leaving space in conversations for others to share their stories rather than dominating with our own
- actively listening to others in a way that shows genuine interest in getting to know them
- looking deeply for that which binds us rather than focusing on what divides us
- parking our judgment and being unconditional in our regard for others

Imagine the presence you will have when you apply your learning about communication connectors with your learning about authenticity. This combination can leave an indelible mark on how you present yourself and how you are perceived, and it can infectiously model the way for others.

SHIFTING GEARS IN NAVIGATING CONFLICT

For many of us, the word *conflict* ignites a barrage of negative thoughts and makes us cringe. At the mere hint of conflict, whether it takes the shape of something subtle in body language or a derogatory comment—we position ourselves to do battle, instead of realizing our best collaborations can come from navigating conflict. To reap positive outcomes for both parties and preserve our working relationships, we need to shift gears; that is, reframe how we think about and respond to conflict. This means a paradigm shift in which we move away from viewing conflict as being volatile, destructive, and focused on win-loss outcomes toward viewing conflict as healthy, natural, and productive.

Here are a few tips about how we can begin to reframe conflict:

- **Remind ourselves that conflict is part of life.** At some point in time, we'll disagree with something that is said or done.
- **View conflict as a relationship builder.** Authentic working relationships develop when we candidly share what we think and feel.
- **Think of conflict as a problem that we are invited to solve with another person.** Imagine the possibilities when we start brainstorming!
- **Keep the focus on issues.** Be tough on them but gentle with your colleagues.
- **Have faith in others.** Collectively we can find solutions to problems.

It is in these moments of conflict that the litmus test of communication awaits us. Often, we climb the ladder of inference when we see behaviors or hear remarks which contradict our sense and sensibility. In zero to three seconds we go from composed and confident to responding with raw emotion. This usually leads to a litany of evaluative remarks that back the speaker into a corner and send the conversation spiraling downward into a messy puddle of disengagement. An emotional response of any kind can cloud our ability to remain calm, logical, and grounded in preserving the dignity and respect of others. When emotions surface, they usually send off warning bells that we should politely excuse ourselves from the conversation and return when calmer heads prevail. Perhaps. But when these emotions come flooding forward, a plan is needed to respond in the moment.

When an emotional gremlin invades your ability to concentrate, take a moment to acknowledge it: identify exactly what it is, label how it makes you feel, and then send it to the back of your brain where it belongs. Lock it up! At first, this is difficult to do, yet with practice, you can quell the emotional triggers which threaten to sabotage your ability to be present and to think and respond cogently in the heat of conflict. It is unrealistic to think we can eliminate our emotional triggers; they will always remain a part of who we are, and they can creep into our awareness at any time. However, we can develop a strategy for managing them when they land.

After you have developed skills to put emotions in abeyance, the stage is set for you to step into the conversation with the *inquiry-based* approach to communication, which we discussed earlier. From an *inquiry-based* position, we can better explore how we can partner to remedy the situation at hand and, in doing so, minimize the probability that the same conflict surfaces again.

CONCLUSION OR BEGINNING?

There is a teachable moment in every conversation we have with others. To grow effective in managing connections, take time to reflect on what transpired in your conversations. What do you need to:

- ▶ continue doing because it is constructive and supports a culture of multigenerational collaboration and inclusivity?
- ▶ stop doing because it is counterproductive to engaging well with others?
- ▶ start doing because fostering workplace connections is ongoing work-in-progress?

I envision you at work in the years to come, exercising your exemplary leadership and managing the many challenges and opportunities you face leading forward and leading by example. Armed with a few new tools, you will partner with others to choreograph a culture of multigenerational unity where we connect in extraordinarily semi-perfect ways. With heaps of patience, an unfaltering commitment to doing things differently, and a willingness to be immensely courageous and curious, stretch into a new reality of what your organization can look like. It's just the beginning.

BIBLIOGRAPHY

Alsop, R. (2013). Managing global millennials: put your stereotypes aside, Generation Work, June 6, 2013. Retrieved from http://www.bbc.com/capital/story/20130530-managing-millennials/1

Artley, J. B. & Macon, M. (2009). Can't we all just get along? A review of the challenges and opportunities in a multigenerational workforce. International Journal of Business Research, 9(6), 90–94.

Barford, N. I. & Hester, P. T. (2011). Analysis of generation Y workforce motivation using multi-attribute utility theory. A Publication of the Defense Acquisition, University of Virginia.

Beeson, J. (2009). Why you didn't get that promotion. Harvard Business Review, 87(6), 101–105.

Berkowitz, N. E., & Schewe, D. S. (2011). Generational cohorts hold the key to understanding patients and health care providers: Coming-of-age experiences influence health care behaviors for a lifetime. Marketing Quarterly, 28, 190–204.

Burmeister, M. (2008). From Boomers to Bloggers. Fairfax, VA: Synergy Press.

Crumpacker, M. & Crumpacker, J. M. (2007). Succession planning and generational stereotypes: Should HR consider age based values and attitudes a relevantfactor or a passing fad? Public Personnel Management, 36(4), 349–369.

Gilburg, D. (2008). They're gen y and you're not. CIO, 21(8), 40–43.

Glass, A. (2007). Understanding generational differences for competitive success. Industrial and Commercial Training, 39(2), 98–103.

Good, T., Farley, C. Tambe, H., & Cantrell, S. (2015). *Trends reshaping the future of HR*. Retrieved from http://www.accenture.

com/us-en/Pages/insightfuture-of-hr-trends-digital-radically-disrupts-hr. aspx?c=str_ustandowotfpsgs&n=HR_-_US&KW_ID=szuHOpmO6_dc|pcrid|63120442758

Gursoy, D., Maier, T. A., & Chi, C. G. (2008). Generational differences: An examination of work values and generational gaps in the hospitality workforce. International Journal of Hospitality Management, 27, 448–458.

Howe, N. & Strauss, W. (2000). Millennials Rising: The Next Greatest Generation. New York: Vintage Books.

Hulyk, T. (2015). Marketing to gen z: Uncovering a new world of social media influencers. Franchising World, 32, 34.

Lamm, E. & Meeks, M. D. (2009). Workplace fun: The moderating effects of generational differences. Employee Relations, 31(6), 613–631.

Lipkin, N. & Perrymore, A. (2009). Y in the Workplace: Managing the "Me First" Generation. Franklin Lakes, NJ: Career Press.

Lyons, S. T., Duxbury, L., & Higgins, C. An empirical assessment of generational differences in basic human values. Psychological Reports, 101(2), 339–352.

Martin, C. (2005). From high maintenance to high productivity: What managers need to know about GenY. Industrial and Commercial Training, 37(1), 39–44.

Martin, C. & Tulgan, B. (2002). Managing the Generation Mix. New York: HRD Press.

Montana, P. & Petit, F. (2008). Motivating generation X and Y on the job and preparing Z. Global Journal of Business Research. 2(2), 139–148.

Palley, W. (2012). Gen Z: Digital in their DNA. New York, NY: Thompson. Retrieved from http://www.jwtintelligence.com/wpcontent/uploads

Renfrow, A. (2012). *Meet generation z*. Retrieved from: http://gettingsmart.com/2012/12/meetgeneration-z/

Rideout, V. J., Foehr, U. G., & Roberts, D. F. (2010). *Generation M2: Media in the lives of 8–18 year olds*. Menlo Park, CA: Kaiser Family Foundation. Retrieved from http://kaiserfamilyfoundation.files. word press, com/2013/01/8010.pdf Generation Z: Technology and Social Interest 113

Strauss, W. & Howe, N. (1991). Generations: The History of America's Future. New York: Morrow and Company.

Strutton, D., Taylor, G. D., & Thompson, K. (2011). Investigating generational differences in e-WOM behaviors for advertising purposes, does X = Y? International Journal of Advertising, 30(4), 559-586.

Toronto, E. (2009). Time out of mind: Dissociation in the virtual world. Psychoanalytic Psychology, 26(2), 117–133.

Tulgan, B. (2012, June 26). High-maintenance Generation Z heads to work. *USA Today*. Retrieved from http://usatoday30.usatoday.com/news /opinion/forum/story/2012-06-27/generation-z-work-millennials-social -media-graduates/55845098/1

Zemke, R., Raines, C., & Filipczak, B. (2000). Generations at Work: Managing the clash of Veterans, Boomers, Xers, and Nexters in your workplace. Washington, DC: American Management Association.

INTEGRATED WELFARE SYSTEMS AND DISCLOSURE: APPROACHING EMERGING ISSUES

Maria Teresa Bianchi

Department of "Diritto ed Economia delle attività produttive"
Sapienza University of Rome, Italy

The aim of this essay is to investigate the integrated welfare and disclosure by proposing emerging issues in the contemporary scenario. Following a theoretical approach, the essay proposes a conceptual study introducing an updated literature analysis. In this way, the implications of the essay are directed to academic communities and policymakers.

Keywords: welfare, integrated welfare disclosure, sociability, social responsibility, social statements.

INTRODUCTION AND RESEARCH QUESTION

The social state is a complex system founded on the substantial equality principle and directed toward reducing inequality by means of synergic interventions such as health assistance, public education, unemployment insurance, access to cultural resources (libraries, museums, free time, etc.), old age and invalidity assistance, defense of natural environment. In line with this, the article 2 of the Italian Constitution states that the Republic guarantees: *"the fulfillment of mandatory obligations with regards to political, economic, and social solidarity."*

The most recent demographic and socioeconomic changes have transformed social security systems around the Western world. Globalization and the strict interdependency of economies on the international context have rendered the scenarios in which governments are called upon daily to protect the citizen even more complex. The impact of economic recession seems to have risked the fundamental solidarity principle on which the entire social state relies on, not only in our country.

The necessity to save money on public spending influences services and allows for the identification and activation of tools and intervention for the improvement of citizens' quality of life. In this way, it must place importance on both a legislative and business prospective—for subsidiary welfare, intended as all services that can be offered by public and private institutions to support new needs in social policies.

Thus, this essay's purpose is to investigate emerging issues on the integrated welfare systems and its disclosure and propose an updated conceptualization of the topic in the international context. In fact, company welfare is represented as internal sociability, while environmental protection or innovation can be interpreted as external sociability, representing the uses of resources that a company does not incur costs, but demonstrates its health and social responsibility.

The research methodology uses a qualitative approach and secondary sources to propose to the scientific community a literature analysis.

The research question is: *Which are emerging issues on the integrated welfare and its disclosure?*

The structure of the essay is the following. After the introduction proposes the purpose of the research, the following sections contain the literature analysis, describing emerging issues and implications.

The last section illustrates the final consideration, limitations, and future perspectives of the study.

SUPPLEMENTARY WELFARE AND WELFARE MIX PHENOMENON

Today, the welfare state system has progressively been replaced by a supplementary or subsidiary welfare system, handled by private operators and no longer by the state, which can no longer handle the weight.

The actual historical phase is often described as a "state welfare crisis," tied to the progressive reduction of financial resources available, the adjustment of the socio-sanitary services system, and the overload from bureaucratic ties. This leads to a welfare system that cannot handle the demands of society. The lack of adequate protection has become particularly evident following social changes over the past decades, which have generated new needs amongst citizens and require innovative answers both direct and efficient.

Since the public services system cannot handle the growing needs of society, mechanisms have arisen from private regulation for the satisfaction of needs: we must think about the phenomenon of home nurses, the normalization of babysitting, and the growing request for healthcare assistants for hospitalized patients as well as the placement of the immigrant workforce.

The necessity to save on public spending that sometimes influences services makes it even more necessary to identify and activate tools and interventions for the improvement of citizens' quality of life. So, it must place growing importance—both from a legislative perspective and an entrepreneurial perspective—on subsidiary welfare, intended as all the services that can be offered by public or private institutions to help with new needs in social policies. Private companies must adapt to the loss of welfare by creating new services for their employees and their families, such as healthcare policies, conventions, support for children's education and daycare. Today supplementary welfare is moving in three different directions:

- the financial sector, directed to the concession of mortgages and loans.
- the youth social activities sector, promoting cultural growth and helping with the insertion in the workplace, through academic and professional training deemed adequate. This takes place with a scholarship, master's program, postgraduate studies, stages in companies, or professional specialization courses. The young can also secure financing for trips in Italy and abroad to further sports activities or the study of foreign languages; they are in institutions that offer economic and organizational support for internships abroad and residences for university study outside local residence;
- the sector for old-age social activities, which guarantees support and protection in the most delicate phases of their lives through health care, organization of summer trips, and hospitality in special residences for those who are no longer self-sufficient.

The actors in supplemental welfare are more and more the exponents of civil society, such as companies and private citizens.

The Italian welfare system has started a progressive transformation phase, based on a vertical subsidiary logic (State-Region-Social Entities), finding at a legislative level its most complete discipline in the Law 328/200 "Framework law for the realization of a supplemental system of interventions and social services," notwithstanding constitutional reforms in section V from 2001. This section concerns programming and financial policies and is based on horizontal subsidiary mechanisms for the management of services mostly mandated to the Third Sector (e.g., welfare mix). Modifications are directed to affirm a welfare society (Vittadini, 2002, Antonini, 2000). The role of the third sector is emergent along with the social company but that for its realization at the moment there are multiple criticalities and gaps. These are tied to both the nature of the subjects operating in the nonprofit sector and the inefficiency of the accreditation system of entities for the issuance of health services (often interpreted as "accreditation of a structure," not capable of assessing the inappropriateness of social services). All this affects the quality of services offered.

The welfare mix model places itself, in fact, halfway between the centered models and that which confides to the market its spontaneous regulation, as it is oriented to a plurality of subjects involved and a multiplicity of services offered.

The state is always requested to handle the task of setting the rules, setting up incentive mechanisms as well as system checks.

Consequently, on the one hand, the state's responsibility for a set of social rights has remained unchanged, on the other hand, it appears to have mutated the methods through which it does so. Indeed, such a mutation is determined not only by the needs of compensation (since social rights increase but resources available diminish) but by the full realization of the essence of the democratic pluralist state, that generates a multiplicity of emerging forces in society, free to operate even due to the satisfaction of social rights.

This opening, already present in the Italian Constitution from 1948, has received new impulse in legislative evolution (Law 328/2000) and from the reform in section V of the Constitution. Both changes spring from a reassessment of intervention levels closer to citizens (based on the subsidiary principle in its vertical and horizontal meanings). The test of constitutional laws shows that the welfare mix system finds a legal framework as its most profound fundamental.

The necessity of saving on public spending influences services, rendering the identification and activation of tools necessary as well as intervention for the improvement of citizens' quality of life. It can place a growing emphasis—in both legislative and business realms—on subsidiary welfare, intended as the services that can be offered by public and private institutions to support new news in social policy.

Therefore, we are increasingly feeling the need to have a company welfare system representing a founding tool for corporate responsibility. In the current scenario, development of company welfare is no longer considered optional. It has become an essential factor for growth and success in a company.

It is based on the shared principle of sustaining growth, at every level, from a social responsibility intended as an obligation of all the subjects involved, each in relation to their proper role, to integrate social, ethical, and environmental themes in their activities and in their internal and external relationships, operating responsibly, with the knowledge of proper rights and obligations. The approach adopted starts with awareness that from this stage the Social State can no longer guarantee the current levels of protection faced with today's demand and expectation of people in terms of welfare that is growing in quantity and quality.

The creation of a company welfare system is realized through the development of company negotiations that take into consideration the social responsibility, as the possibility of undertaking a "pact" in which parties can formalize their obligation to sustain behavior and coherent choices in industrial relations for development of a socially responsible company (Lindgreen, Swaen, 2010).

The choices in social responsibility shared in negotiations represent, within the realm of the agreement, the "welfare negotiations," constituting regulations formalized to give answers to the needs of workers and their families, in sections with social relevance. Through such agreements, they respond, therefore, to tangible individual and/or family necessities that represent a recognized need for collectivity.

The choices and behavior oriented toward social responsibility in industrial relations and company negotiations suppose sharing from all the actors involved to favor, at the company level, the adoption of socially responsible choices. Voluntary sharing and awareness of such choices in company negotiations can contribute to spreading sensitivity and culture on social responsibility issue, promoting ethical behavior and improving relations between companies and local communities.

The company assumes a substantial and effective role. Companies have been capable of gathering the most varied needs of their workers constructing, in many cases, an exemplary model for supplemental welfare.

The phenomenon of company welfare is a sure sign of the diffusion of a new sensitivity of companies, always more conscious of the needs of company workers in terms of strategic advantage directed to increase productivity and company competitiveness.

In this way, the investigation is directed to understand the role of companies. The state can no longer deal with pressuring requests for welfare that are coming from workers, male and female, retired pensioners, and aspiring workers.

Companies must have a more active role, but how? The recession that is not allowing the state to fulfill its welfare obligations is the same that is putting pressure on companies. Therefore?

The first answer is related to the company as a container of social services. This is evident when the company is managed economically: "reaching economic objectives with minimal costs, without waste and with attention to future perspective."

We must start from future perspective to explain the significance of creating a series of conditions that allow for the realization of so-called "internal social policies" or company welfare, based on the logic of the companies social responsibility.

To realize such objectives, companies must collect resources. They cannot create such resources outside, due to the economic/social historical period. They must find them internally. Self-financing (Capaldo, 1968) also relates to resources generated internally, that, in terms of company savings, allow for the creation of resources to designate for social use in the strictest sense of company welfare.

If the companies, *rectius* the businessmen, would begin to consider designating internal resources for social use and that this, would increase (and not decrease) the value of the company, as it is even more recognized on an international scale, then we can hypothesize a common interest of the actors in collective negotiations. A model socially responsible company is that which takes charge to create conditions to guarantee a future to its company, and therefore its workers, to its country and naturally to the businessman.

It is what financial analysts ask for, integrating financial *ratings* with the non-financial ones of essentially social or ethical nature.

From here, the importance of social reporting and the assessment of socioeconomic capital, through forms of "social correction" of values. derive from an evaluation of patrimonial/financial/economic nature.

Going back to company welfare models, the models are not new, and the most cited case is the Olivetti model represented below.

FROM THE OLIVETTI MODEL TO THE CURRENT MODEL

The company Olivetti has covered a key role in Italian industrial life not only in its performance with regards to technology and economics but also due to the attention it pays to its employees and their problems.

Adriano Olivetti has succeeded his father, the founder of the company. Camillo Olivetti had a vision: a company had to create not only that value which is distributed to the shareholders in terms of benefits but also that which was invested to self-finance the company. Therefore Olivetti would be generous in its salaries, incentives for work obligations, social and assistance services for employees, permanent training, and even reduction of work hours with the same salaries for staff.

Adriano Olivetti followed the strategy of becoming a "big company" because in this manner can it respond to all its potential future economic opportunities (Maggia, 2001), so under his leadership, the company went from 200 employees in 1924 to 4,000 in 1942 and 25,000 in 1961.

He also emphasized the importance of innovation technology, by introducing product designers with high scientific preparation in industrial activities, where the old collaborators with his father, whom the company had sacrificed much to develop, had to step aside and make room for the cum laude graduates in mechanics, electromechanics, and electronics (Olivetti, 1958).

Adriano Olivetti urged the company to be international and compete in more international markets to maintain itself as large and powerful; in the 1930s and 1940s, it created foreign subsidiaries in Belgium, Argentina, Spain, Brazil, and France. When Adriano Olivetti passed away, it had production offices in Italy (in Canavese, in Turin, in Massa and Pozzuoli), Europe (Barcellona and Glasgow), Latin America (Buenos Aires and San Paulo), and the United States (Hartford).

Adriano Olivetti followed a corporate culture to the end; sustaining, as early as 1945, the necessity to " give awareness to then ends of work" (Olivetti, 1960), asking that "industry could reach certain ends where they could find profit indicators or if there were beyond any apparent return, something more fascinating, an ideal story, a destination, a vocation in the factory"

Finally, Adriano Olivetti established strong ties with the "factory" and the territory in which it was settled; he created a series of accessible services for all the population, not only the employees and their families, as in the Social Relations Centre and the Olivetti Cultural Centers. He also founded the I-RUR, an institute for urban and rural renovation in Canavese. It had the objective of studying and executing programs on a communal and inter-communal basis, to improve social and economic conditions of the region, the standard of life and the cultural level of the population, to give contributions to the full employment of labor and to promote, create and manage concrete industrial, agricultural and artisan activities.

Olivetti can be considered the paradigm of the company welfare system, as cultivated by both the father Camillo and the son Adriano. Its factory was not only a place of work finalized to the production of goods but above all an environment for social coexistence.

The first social activities were established in 1909 together with Workshop, with the creation of a mutual fund to assist skilled workers, to guarantee the employees medical and economic assistance in case of injury in the workplace or tuberculosis. At first, the mutual funds did not work very well: a worker to be hospitalized would have to pass all his medical information to the main city of the province, who would pass it to Rome and, about three months would go by before such information would be sent back with clearance.

In 1919, anticipating the legislative dispositions on the subject, the company instituted a family indemnity of 12 lire for each dependent child for all its employees. The practice of family indemnity continued and, in 1949, it brought about the creation of a plan of integrated family indemnity alongside those issued by INPS (AA.VV., *2001*).

In 1924, in response to the increase in skilled workers and bad living conditions, Olivetti began construction of apartments for its employees.

In 1932, Adriano took over for his father in the management of the company and brought about many new changes. Before 1936, Olivetti offered personal assistance to every worker, while later it adopted a more structured assistance policy, which Adriano defined as a "welfare system," based on the idea that workers could use assistance and services set up by the company while supplying their skills at the service of the company. The employees acquired rights from the policy in the vision of *"do ut des"* and not for charity. The employees found themselves with a daycare center, summer retreats, and factory services (cafeteria, automobile services, and repairs for transport vehicles). They built schools to teach professional design, such as the Olivetti School, the Centre for Mechanics Training, and the Technical Industrial Institute, with scholarship mechanisms allowing young people with technique to become head technicians or engineers. They organized cultural services (Olivetti Cultural Centre, conferences, theater shows, cinema, art shows, and concerts) and training (libraries, night courses for employees). The establishment of centers for social services had two purposes: on the one hand, it was a promotional tool for the economic and social wellness of the company, and on the other hand, it meant avoiding conflicts and tensions between management and the worker class, in a historical phase characterized by a notable increase in manpower. Policies were promoted with regards to maternity and children; in 1934, the company built its first daycare center with an attached pediatric service to it. In 1941, Olivetti enacted Worker's Assistance Regulations that recognized more advantageous economic treatment than what the law provided, with regards to maternity leave, the conservation of job post for nine months, almost paid fully. The economic and structural growth of the company placed more and more at the center of its discussion the living conditions of its staff. To resolve this issue after the war, it built new neighborhoods based on modern urban schemes, such as Borgo Olivetti, Canton Vesco, Montemarano, Bellavista. Loans, as well as sureties, were granted, and technical consultancy as well as architectural was free for all its employees. The intense construction activities dealt with the completion of the factory in Ivrea, the construction of a Study Center, the design of a cafeteria, school, theater, hospital in Ivrea, third bridge in Ivrea, and the factories labeled I-RUR58.

Since 1948, the company's social services institute has been managed by the Management Council, an instrument created to render the workers directly participant to social assistance in the factories. An example of the Council's works is the Internal Solidarity Fund, which employees finance with a monthly contribution and which gives aid in the case of sickness or injury by integrating with the national social security system.

Hiring policies were characterized by recruiting more members in the family nucleus to increase consumer and saving capabilities and impede wild urbanization of the territory. According to the archives on personnel, 80 percent of staff hired to work in Olivetti from 1924 to 1960 continued to live in the same municipalities, thanks to the efficient, low-cost transport system and subsidized loans for home renovation. Even if the number of employees grew enormously in this period, passing from 200 to 10,000, Ivrea only grew by 5,000 inhabitants, and the remaining part of Canavese retained the same population numbers.

For their responsible company policies tied to the territory, Adriano Olivetti clashed both with Confindustria and worker's unions because of work hours' reduction without a change in salary, as his ideas seemed always to anticipate theirs with regards to welfare.

Adriano Olivetti understood before others that the two tools that let a company operate efficiently were scientific organization for production—associated with the acquisition and use of specialized plants—and social management of its workforce to add value to proximity relations between the company and its environment. Employee wellness, in fact, guaranteed lasting conditions for the success of the company. For this reason, the company undertook a series of activities for social development, such as the construction of health centers furnished with convalescents and qualified doctors for its employees and their families, in order to block the diffusion of epidemics or debilitating diseases like tuberculosis, and the creation of employee cafeterias to fight the health food problem in that period.

Olivetti was not the only company in those years to adopt a company welfare system. Other companies, even in more recent times, have done so. For example, the welfare policies of Martini & Rossi (Napoleone Rossi di Montelera: *"the profit could not be separated from the economic and social growth of those who worked in the company"*) have assistance policies, such as the availability of day care for its employees. From the beginning, this offered a series of advantages to workers with very young children during work (in normal daycare schools, children are admitted at three years of age) and after work (with the organization of trips, cultural visits, sports competitions and musical events). Other family benefits included female creative organization and the summer colonies where the children of employees could spend vacation periods (between the 1930s and the 1950s, in the Martini houses in the Alps, in Valle d'Aosta and then at the end of the 1990s, in a new property in Salice d'Ulzio). Martini & Rossi even put a true construction policy into effect at the beginning of the 1950s and 1960s in favor of its employees. It activated such policies to supply good living at a low cost to employees; and so, without a coherent development, it established numerous "employee houses" furnished with spacious apartments and rational living quarters.

In a more recent period, how can we not recall company welfare policies in Pirelli, with their initiatives regarding assistance and family support; Luxottica, with regard to health and wellness, education and merit promotion, mobility and social assistance; ENI, with initiatives for the family, health, and initiatives for time and money savings; or Intesa San Paolo, with complimentary social security, complimentary/supplemental health insurance, free time in recreational centers, and solidarity?

BINOMIAL ECONOMICS AND SOCIABILITY

In the past years, following globalization, an issue has emerged related to economic themes, ethical problems, and corporate social responsibility (McWilliams, 2000; McIntosh, 2003; Lindgreen, Swaen, 2010). In the 1930s, company economics researchers amplified their research toward corporate behavior by considering consequences of company activities on the social collectivity (Donham, 1927). The discussion is started by the socially responsible managerial class, capable of orienting its behavior in a socially responsible manner. Sociability appears as a primary factor in avoiding the decline of companies (Donham, 1927).

Today, social functions in the company system (Carroll, 1999) are even more relevant, due to the growth in maturity of our civil society that has elevated its requests and expectations toward public and private institutions, to which a request is made to find a balance between economic criteria and social finality in the governance of activities carried out. In the 1950s, studies began to identify additional objectives concerning financial economics, to be found in social actions directed toward the company (Bowen, 1953). In the 1960s, many studies began to ask if companies could allow themselves to not consider social responsibility with regards to their actions (Davis, 1960; McGuire, 1963; Walton, 1967). From the Freidman theories (Friedman, 1970) that social responsibility could not fail in profit growth, an idea emerged of a relationship between higher profits and greater responsibility. Often such a binomial is correlated to company productivity. The sociability issue is therefore connected to having found many ideas in an era of globalization. In fact, social issues are related to the discussion elements in all sectors. Public awareness covers such relevant aspects as unemployment, environmental protection and worker's protection and the transformation of consumer markets due to continuous changes dictated by the collectivity and new habits in potential consumers. We have seen the radicalization of the binomial between rich countries and developing countries, with "new entries" in these countries' new age (Bianchi, 2010).

SOCIAL STATEMENTS
A Different Approach to Social Statements

Sociability has relevance if it is directed and accountable to the outside. From this simple assumption studies and applications (Wood, 1993) have led to the creation of social accounting, through forms of *social accountability*.

Corporate management has inevitable social implications that transcend corporate action observed from a classic point of view or, rather, set up to assess economic-financial implications.

Social information is always more relevant for the assessments that the markets permit the company. We have already stated that the study presented by Advantage Financial explains the reasons for better access to credit for companies that adopt socially responsible policies. Traditional models for reporting don't demonstrate the methods with which companies create and use policies for social actions. In other words, these models are efficient under a descriptive profile but don't quantify the social phenomenon. The goal of a social statement is to explain how resources are created and used, and the models mentioned do not allow for a correct analysis of this topic.

From this perspective, monitoring and measuring social actions by companies through self-financing is relevant.

Self-financing (or company savings) is an economic phenomenon with financial effects allowing for minor recourse to credit capital to use internal company resources for new investments. This allows for an increase in future performance and ensures vitality and growth. Such a role is even more evident when self-financing is used to invest in research and development, marketing, safeguarding of the environment, and accident prevention.

In this way, there is a positive valuation of the indicators ACE (economic growth aid), or rather a tax incentive that is recognized to companies who decide to save and invest the company savings with an "industrial" perspective. Self-financing is fed through the waiver of shareholders on their dividends, which means, even under an ethical profile, the waiver of cashing in profits to increase company development represents socially responsible corporate behavior.

In this direction, the following section explains how a social statement model can be built on self-financing.

Social Statement Based on the Self-Financing Model

To communicate its sociability, a company uses social statements. The general aim of social statements is to describe the reasons for sustaining costs that are uncharacteristic but productive for stakeholders. They go alongside financial statements and complete them with evaluation and reporting of aspects that are not monetary with regards to company performance.

In the past years, there has been a growth in awareness of the way companies produce and how they use up environmental, social and economic resources. Sustainability has become the main evaluation term for companies and public administrations that want to take on a socially responsible role.

Today this tool is relevant for the company system, in fact, "social information must be produced with rigor and accounting methodology," and "the judicial subjects must feel the obligation, or be obligated, to supply punctual information on what their social obligations are, with reference to the internal and external environments of the company" (Bianchi, 2010).

Economic research must be, more than ever, realized based on an ethical paradigm.

The social statement is a summary analysis of the reasons for sustaining costs, not immediately referable to specific activities, but capable of generating advantages for stakeholder categories (such as personnel, shareholders, investors, clients, users, suppliers, public administrations, and society as a whole).

The construction of a social statement can be based on three profiles: identification of content, internal coherence of content, and process. In fact, the different types of social statements proposed by various organizations refer to guidelines (Global Reporting Initiative, a study group for regulating preparation principles for social statements, self-financing) and process (AccountAbility 1000). The guidelines involve the structure and meaning of the report, to analyze the relation's network on which quality depends on for the results of government action. Process standards are concentrated primarily on the construction mechanism of the report and propose some phases each finalized with an outcome explaining which principles are used for the preparation.

So we propose an innovative model, described in doctrine and applied in practice by emphasizing the uses of earned proceeds.

The Innovative Model of Analysis

The social statement for self-financing as innovative model is the tool that best allows for the description of company sociability due to investments of "company savings."

This social statement model is composed of two parts: the social statement in a strict sense, with a comparison between resources and uses as seen below, and comments used to explain the otherwise quantitative data.

RESOURCES	USES
1 Self-financing of the report:	3 Internal Sociability:
1.1 retained earnings (profit net of dividends)	3.1 Development & research costs
1.2 provisions	3.2 Training personnel costs
1.3 depreciations	3.3 prevention devices
2 Rectifications:	4 External sociability:
2.1 for price policies	4.1 installations for minor environmental impact
2.2 for tax policies	4.2 marketing expenses
	Asset reinforcement over a long-term period
TOTAL RESOURCES (1+2)	**TOTAL USES (3+4)**

The comments on the social statements concern resources exposed in the scheme, explain the quantitative data expressed in the table, and allow reconstruction of the voice for self-financing of the statement and uses. Comments emphasize the value of social investments both internally and externally. Such data primarily emerges from a comparison of the patrimonial state of the statement's year-end with the one from the previous year.

This model of social statement begins from self-financing, as the summary of profits that are not distributed, depreciation, and provisions calculated net of utility funds is a good indicator of social potential, even better than traditional indicators such as employment and taxes.

Social potential is represented by an elevated propensity to save, and therefore invest, in order to significantly improve the company's economic prospects. It seems evident that company savings can represent social potential, and therefore self-financing indicates a positive economic outcome capable of expressing a relation between external and internal environments. In fact, "self-financing represents a true tool for the evaluation of action, as it results from rational management, it has the seed of the future, thus establishing itself as a true social resource."

Currently, a *credit crunch* impedes companies in their growth, especially small to average-sized companies, having financing, financial autonomy needs to be increased. In other words, companies are less dependent on the market and can, therefore, handle investments with means generated inside the company system. Self- financing is a measure of resources that a company and its management can generate on its own.

The model for self-financing contains some peculiarities that describe a series of social actions: the first is price policy. In fact, the model reads price policies with a strong discount as an additional resource. This is clear in technical accounting terms: minor prices/ higher profits, very true in terms of sociability. A maintenance policy of prices today represents a social resource for companies, allowing them to meet their clients halfway. In food distribution and large consumer goods, today a price policy and tariff policies are among elements having a broad social impact.

The referred model divides the social uses into internal and external uses. This means using the potential derived from self-financing for sociability to reward internal and external stakeholders.

This leads to the quantification of company welfare as mentioned at the beginning of the essay. In other words, companies invest in actions directed toward improvement of work conditions of their employees, and they also invest in the external environment, but companies also invest in innovation, and this improves their products and processes so that they can release products on the market with even less environmental impact.

The self-financing model quantifies social action, but it is the model that has further value. In fact, self-financing is an indicator of the company's state of health. It is easy to demonstrate that companies, whatever size, tend to generate self-financing based on their capacities and limits in their sector of activities (the marginality of every company and every sector is different). This postulates that self-financing is a pure social resource and its use is a modality to understand how it realizes socially responsible actions.

Internal sociability coincides with all the tools for company welfare that have been mentioned, while external sociability represents the actions of a company toward the outside, and therefore, all innovation-realized sociability improves environmental impact.

"Innovation is defined with the social process through which an invention or a creative idea is adopted by a group . . . This is the moment in which the initial idea has a social fall –out and contributes to the progress of humanity" (Sinibaldi, 2012).

It is recognized as the primary motor for the economic and social growth of a nation (available at www.ilsole24ore.com) favoring productivity and therefore increases in GDP, increase in quality and variety of products offered and duration of social wellness (Franzini et al., 2012). Strong ties exist between innovation and sociability.

CSR-*oriented* initiatives can generate innovation through the use of social, environmental and sustainable *drivers* used to create new products, services, and processes capable of triggering, through *networking,* a virtuous circle.

The relation between CRS and innovation is revealed with more force in organizations where corporate social responsibility is an integrated part of company strategy. In this regard, it is useful to distinguish those who have a reactive approach to change from those that have a proactive approach. While a reactive approach is not capable of anticipating change, and so it can only use a reaction plan with effects in the short term, who has a proactive approach perceives the tendencies in advance and is capable of creating a new action plan and generating innovation that is sustainable over time.

SUMMARY AND CONCLUSIONS
Summarizing Economics and Sociability

This section demonstrates a synthesis between economics and sociability. The concept of economics, or rather the capacity of a company to reach objectives as in minimum costs and no waste of resources with attention to the future perspective, shows how such attention does not have to be directed only to making profits. It can also be directed to creating economic capital conditions to allow the company's sustainable development.

The company that wants to orient its management to sociability principles can do it without undermining its profits or company development.

The objective that arises is spontaneous, above all in a global economy, to safeguard profit, development, and sociability. The company that delocalizes in countries where workforce and prime goods have a lower cost seem to have an advantage in global competition. So why consider sociability?

Companies that have developed their own business without asking themselves about future perspectives, even with a social outlook, today are squashed from excessive debt or scarcity of quality, which costs them appeal to customers.

Sustainable growth, even in social terms, allows them to remain on the market. Innovation (Chesbrough, 2010; Gollin, 2008; Teece, 2010) is the key to success. It enables the realization of products with minor impact and major efficiency. It is the case to observe in a mature market how the automobile industry has found new life due to innovation allowing for growth of the product's lifecycle.

The key to innovation analysis is the medium-long-term period as the element of the social environment. The concept of economics refers to future perspectives, "compelling" the businessman to a type of management that not only tends toward maximization of performance contingencies but also deals with obtaining positive long-term results. It is evident that company investment in innovation will waive immediate profits to improve future economic-financial results, generate development, and socioenvironmental progress.

Today's successful and innovative company needs to compete. We also need to consider the impacts operations will have on society and the environment, stimulating the creativity of personnel and collaborating with *stakeholders* in designing and developing new products and services. It is necessary not to equate innovation with technological evolution but diffuse into the conscience of every company, of every size, the idea that innovation must be a continuous activity as well as systematic to involve all *business units*. (MacGregor, Fontrodona, 2008).

Conclusions on the Role of the Company in New Welfare

Following the previous theoretical analysis, companies must act as primary creators of social wellness.

Traditional welfare has receded due to the abovementioned considerations; thus, the third sector manages the most requests: the state doesn't, and no other operator can fill the role. Think about nonprofit organizations that qualify personnel who are prisoners or ex-prisoners. This absolves the Constitutional concept since it provides for rehabilitation of the penalty. Such activity cannot be the answer to a social security system that can longer give answers to employees and workers. It can no longer create conditions for more active participation of women in the workplace in all levels of responsibility. Therefore, the Third Sector, which has considerable merit, cannot be loaded down with an activity structured in terms of welfare. So, companies become active in this new welfare model that is starting to outline itself.

The resources that companies designate to such activities are to be found in self-financing as resources that the company saves, of whatever size, that it can always generate. Company welfare is interpreted as internal sociability, just as environmental protection or innovation can be interpreted as external sociability, representing the uses of resources in which a company does not incur costs, but demonstrates its health and social responsibility.

Especially when you go to promote the attention of rating agencies, banks, funding agencies and so on to evaluate the companies that invest in these activities positively, somehow the circle closes: social media with industry-funded self-generated and with the benefit of positive appeal to "spend" in all markets (financial markets, outlet, supply, etc.).

So, there remains a problem of the moral order. The good for the sake of Kantian memory, or the more recent *bonum honestum* of John Paul II, are inevitably factors related to the single individual. Much can be done about this, but not with self-financing or other means of financial nature, but with the search for a scale of values which one needs to go back and use as inspiration. But this is an issue that goes beyond the present research.

REFERENCES

AA.VV., 2001. Speciale per Adriano Olivetti, *L'uomo che visse il futuro*, in La Sentinella del Canavese, Gruppo Editoriale L'Espresso, Ivrea.

Antonini, L., 2000. *Il principio di sussidiarietà orizzontale: da Welfare State a Welfare Society*, in Riv.dir. fin. e sc. fin..

Bianchi, C., 2010. *Strutture aziendali nel mercato globalizzato*, Seconda Edizione, Società Editrice Esculapio, Bologna.

Bowen, H. R., 1953. *Social responsibility of businessmen*, New York, Harper.

Capaldo, P., 1968. *L'Autofinanziamento nell'economia dell'impresa*, Giuffrè, Milano.

Carroll, A. B., 1999. Corporate social responsibility evolution of a definitional construct. *Business & Society*, Vol. 38, No. 3, pp. 268–295.

Chesbrough, H., 2010. "Business model innovation: opportunities and barriers," *Long Range Planning*, Vol. 43, No. 2, pp. 354–363.

Davis, K., 1960. Can business afford to ignore social responsibilities?, *California Management Review*, No. 3.

Donham, W. B., 1927. The social significance of business, *Harvard Business Review*, July.

Franzini, M., Giannini, M., & Zamparelli, L., 2012. *Innovare per crescere—strategie e scelte politiche*, Egea, Milano.

Friedman, M., 1970. The social responsibility of business is to increase its profits, *New York Times Magazine*, n. 13, September.

Gollin, M. A., 2008. *Driving Innovation: IP Strategies for a Dynamic World*. Cambridge University Press, New York.

Lindgreen, A. & Swaen, V., 2010. Corporate social responsibility, *International Journal of Management Reviews*, Vol. 12, No. 1, pp. 1–7.

McWilliams, A., 2000. *Corporate Social Responsibility*, Wiley Encyclopedia of Management.

McIntosh, M., 2003. *Raising a Ladder to the Moon: The Complexities of Corporate Social and Environmental Responsibility*, Palgrave, Basingstoke.

Maggia, G., 2001. *Speciale per Adriano Olivetti, L'uomo che visse il futuro*, in La Sentinella del Canavese, Gruppo Editoriale L'Espresso, Ivrea.

McGuire, J. W., 1963. Business and society, Mac Grow Hill, New York.

Olivetti, A., 1958. *Appunti per la Storia di una fabbrica*, in Musatti R, Bigiaretti, L., Soavi, G., *Olivetti 1908- 1958*, Ing. Olivetti & Company S.p.A., Ivrea, p. 9.

Olivetti, A., 1960. *Discorsi ai lavoratori*, in Città dell'uomo, Edizioni di Comunità, Roma.

Olivetti, A., 1960. *Corrispondenza per gli Stati Uniti*, Edizioni di Comunità, Roma.

Teece, D. J., 2010. *Business Model, Business Strategy, and Innovation*, Long Range Planning, Vol. 43, No. 2, pp. 172-194.

Vittadini, G., 2002. *Liberi di scegliere. Dal welfare State alla welfare society*, Etas, Milano.

Walton, C. C., 1967. *Corporate Social Responsibility*, Belmont, Wadsworth.

Wood, D. J., 1993. *Auditing the market: a practical approach to social auditing*, New Economics Foundation, London.

EDUCATION—"ALFA" AND "OMEGA" FOR DEVELOPMENT

Ineza Gagnidze,
Irina Gogorishvili,
Nino Papachashvili

Doctors of Economics, Associate Professors,
Iv. Javakhishvili Tbilisi State University, Georgia.

In the twenty-first century, technologies turned into intellectual products. The processes of their commercialization should take place at the end of the global crisis. International specialization processes are underway in the production of technologies as well as goods. Their study and analysis are beyond the economic interests and abilities of separate countries. But the convergence of the world and national economic interests is still too weak or nonexistent because of the absence of motivation. Of course, governments, for objective and subjective reasons, will not make independent efforts to create and strengthen motivations. However, they can set up an international organization, motivated from the very start to make global educational and knowledge policy. Establishment of the world organization in the education sphere and definition of the functions and authorities thereof is far more important (it will play a crucial role in human development) than enlargement of authorities of other international organizations.

Generally being four or eight years in power, governments are oriented to short-term results and effects. With these approaches, the formation of effective policy which gives results in the long term shall move to the background. On the one hand, the innovative development of economy requires special attention to the science and education spheres. On the other hand, they are precisely the areas in which the desired results can be achieved only in the long term. For this reason, thinking about the project issues was very interesting for us.

The sound of a separate note in the musical composition is relatively weaker than the accord. For this reason, we believe that the initiation of three ideas simultaneously around the project problems in one work would be more successful than just initiating one. They are:

- ✓ Clusters, entrepreneurial universities and secondary schools—tools for effective local economic policy for the long term;
- ✓ Formation of an effective link between the economic cycle and educational systems;
- ✓ Globalization of markets and the role of SMEs in escaping the "development trap."

METHODOLOGY

For the preparation of this publication, we reviewed the literature about clusters, education and science systems, and competitiveness. One of the primary methods used is the comparison method, both in time (literature review on clusters for the last twenty-six years) and in space (ten countries). To test these hypotheses, we use the case study as an analytical tool, as well as analogy, correlation, and systemic approach. Also, we used the methods of logical analysis, synthesis, and abstraction.

LITERATURE REVIEW

It's widely recognized that education has a significant impact on economic growth and development. This is argued by a number of researchers, in particular: J. A. Shumpeter (1939), N. Kontradieff (1935), S. Kuznets (1973), M. Hirooka (2006), A. Akaev (2009), G. Mensch (2006), A. Korotaev and S. Tsirel (2010), and I. Gogorishvili (2011).

The document of European Commission states, "The specific function of education as the basis of the knowledge triangle needs to be further developed" (2009/C 302/03). The model of the entrepreneurial university that effectively connects education, science, and business appears in H. Etzkowitz and Ch. Zhou (2008), J. G. Wissema (2009), P. Kyrö and J. Mattila (2012), S. M. Awbrey (2003), and M. Guerrero and D. Urbano (2010). The secondary schools and teaching entrepreneurship in them have great importance for the development of the local economy in the long term. We studied the cases of ten countries, based upon the works of I. Hatak and E. Reiner (2011), L. Vestergaard (2015), E. Fredua-Kwarteng (2005), and others.

We discussed the importance of cluster in economic development based upon the works of M. E. Porter (1998; 2008) and Ch. Ketels (2015).

CLUSTERS, ENTREPRENEURIAL UNIVERSITIES, AND SECONDARY SCHOOLS—TOOLS FOR EFFECTIVE LOCAL ECONOMIC POLICY FOR THE LONG TERM

Gottfried Wilhelm Leibniz wrote, "Every present state of a simple substance is the natural consequence of its preceding state, in such a way that its present is big with its future." From this point of view, I had an idea to compare the views expressed in M. Porter's famous work *The Competitive Advantage of Nations* published twenty-six years ago to the current situation and, by estimation, to make proposals for the project topic.

Why were these countries studied twenty-five to thirty years ago? "Together, the ten nations studied accounted for fully 50 percent of total world exports in 1985" (Porter, 1998, p. 21). The cases (Porter, 1998, pp. 26–27) studied by the author still play an important role in the success of their countries economy. Below we will try to explain how these clusters maintained their competitiveness from then until today.

According to the author's definition, "a cluster is a geographically proximate group of interconnected companies and associated institutions in a particular field, linked by commonalities and complementarities. They constitute a forum in which new types of dialogue can, and must, take place among firms, government agencies, and institutions (such as schools, universities, and public utilities)" (Porter M. E., 2008, p. 215).

In his work providing the development of the theory on clusters (after Marshall, Schumpeter, and Becattini (COM (2008) 652 final, p. 7), Porter wrote that determinants of national advantage were crucial for the success of clusters. These were "firm strategy, structure, and rivalry, related and supporting industries, factor conditions and demand conditions" (Porter, 1998, p. 72). At the same time, "the positive and negative roles of government in the process of creating competitive advantage are highlighted and clarified by viewing government as an influencer of the national "diamond" (Porter, 1998, p.128). There are lots of literature on the efficiency of clusters and cluster initiatives in the economy. We would like to mention that we fully agree with Ketels (2015, p. 28), who, based upon many authors' work (Aiginger, 2006; Aghion et al., 2011; Rodrik, 2004; Stiglitz et al., 2013; Warwick, 2013), argued that "cluster-based approaches could become a core tool for a new industrial policy."

He also indicated that a fall phase is characteristic for clusters. So in the 1990s, successful clusters minimized expenditures, reduced risks and failures, and provided innovations with the formation of such universities where education, science, and business were in one sphere. These were the entrepreneurial universities, which became the "Perpendo Mobil" of clusters.

There started active discussions on entrepreneurial universities in the economic literature at the end of the twentieth century, including in the following well-known authors: H. Etzkowitz and Ch. Zhou (2008), J. G. Wissema (2009), P. Kyrö and J. Mattila (2012), S. M. Awbrey (2003), and M. Guerrero and D. Urbano (2010).

Entrepreneurial universities gain strength by showing the best form of competitive advantage of the local economy. This success would be unimaginable without their active relation with the secondary education schools. "There is a broad consensus between EU member states concerning the aims and objectives of Entrepreneurship Education. It is largely agreed among experts that it should no longer just be an extra-curricular activity, but instead should be embedded in the curricula across all educational levels and types" (Hatak & Reiner, 2011, p. 3). "Entrepreneurship education is recognised across Europe as one of the important means of raising the level of creativity and innovation among Europe's future work force" (Vestergaard, 2015, p. 4).

We think that an educational and scientific system for the development of the local economy in any country must respond to the following challenges:

- How to improve its international and local estimated figures.
- How to plan the development of science without weighing on the budget of a particular country and partly fund itself (with studies that lead to products, using the potential of the local economy).
- How to inspire younger entrepreneurs to identify regions' competitive advantages.

These challenges can be partially responded if we answer two more questions:

1. In what form can the secondary school become an effective part of the entrepreneurial university?

2. With this complicity, how to get the desired result after 20–25 years of the involvement of today's young people?

We believe that the achievement of international standards of scholastic education, based upon the interests of the country, must additionally provide:

1. the development of professional orientation in such form (with the standard approach) that will reveal regional economies' potential and assist the students' involvement in this business. Such an approach will formalize informal knowledge in each family living in the region and use it to develop the local economy.
2. active formation of entrepreneurial attitudes in pupils with specially designed school projects to help young people better understand their environment and aim to start their own business.

We fully agree with Fredua-Kwarteng (2005, p. 6) that "entrepreneurial studies as part of the senior secondary school (S.S.S) curricula would have the purpose of developing in students the skills, knowledge, and attitudes necessary for starting, running a business and introducing innovations to create new products and markets."

We add that the effective implementation of the abovementioned approach will be possible when the education and science policy is designed for synergy (Gagnidze and Maisuradze (2016)).

FORMATION OF AN EFFECTIVE LINK BETWEEN THE ECONOMIC CYCLE AND EDUCATIONAL SYSTEMS

Wave-like alternation of economic growth and decline lies in the nature of the driving forces (implies aspiration of the capital to maximization of the profit) of the market itself. In 1912, world-famous economist Joseph Schumpeter indicated that the scientific-technical innovations were the main driving forces of economic development. He wrote that when innovation is inculcated in economics, "creative destruction" takes place, fundamentally unbalancing the current economic system (Shumpeter, 1939).

It conditions extinguishing of old technologies, fields and organizational structures, replacing them with new fields and institutional capacities. It results in unprecedented dynamism of economic development, which Schumpeter called the "Orchestra van effect." In his opinion, investments without innovations are meaningless and even harmful as they are, in effect, use of capital that impedes economic activity (Shumpeter, 1934).

Russian scientist N. Kontradieff developed a theory about comparative dynamics of industrial conjuncture, which he called the long cycle (wave) theory of 40/60s (Kondratieff, 1935). Along with the long waves by Kondratieff, there are fewer time cycles theories formulated by the scientists Kuznets, Juglar, and Kitchin (Korotaev and Tsirel, 2010).

The "Depression Trigger Effect" developed by Gerhard Mensch implies that the different basic innovations (nano, bio, informational, and cognitive technologies (NBIC)), via the self-organization mechanism, create clusters and are revealed in the depression phase. Depressed economic agents are forced to seek solutions "offered" by the establishment of innovations; therefore, a new depression triggers this establishment. Clusters of basic technologies create new fields and further develop the technological cycle of Kondratieff's long period (Mensch, 2006).

The formation of advantages of the innovational development, called the innovational paradigm by the Japanese scientist Hirooka (2006), consists of three logistic trajectories: technology, enactment, and diffusion. The trajectory of technology is attributed to the unity of basic technologies, classified as innovation. Enactment trajectory represents the unity of new innovative products, obtained by the application of new basic technologies. It plays a vital role in innovational paradigm since it is the area for transmission of technologic knowledge from academic institutions to the entrepreneurial sector (given utilization of innovational products and further commercialization thereof). Favorable conditions for venture enterprises are being formed during the first ten to fifteen years of the trajectory. Hence, it is of utmost importance for us to maintain the best opportunities during this period for the commercialization of innovations. The trajectories of technology and diffusion have as well been for the first time studied by Hirooka, defining their duration as twenty-five to thirty years. Thus, the innovational paradigm he surveyed is of the cascade structure and consists of three logistic trajectories, lagging behind each other with the fixed interval of time defined by empiric means.

Some innovations during the transition to the new technological cycle entail the creation of new infrastructures and networks, facilitating the formation of long-term trends of development. Hereof main (axial) innovations, at the initial stage of distribution, create new markets, but their further enlargement generates new infrastructure in economics (Hirooka, 2006, p. 426.). Such infrastructure creates the networks (for logistics of factors), which also provides formation of a well-defined cluster with the main, axial innovation. Informational technologies were considered as hereof innovations before crisis (Akaev & Hirooka, 2009). In their turn, main innovations entail different inventions and institutional changes, which further condition enlargement of markets in the technological cycle. Social and technological innovations in countries and regional integrations within new technological cycles shall be ongoing in simultaneous mode. This is the only way to obtain synergy.

The main economic characteristic of the new technological cycle is particularly noteworthy—**globalization of increasing effect process of production scale**, which is differentiated according to countries and fields.

Developed countries specialize in scientific fields (according to the vital cycle theory of the product) based on global processes, which provide increasing effects of scale. Large companies, based on the cooperation process, create venture companies in developing countries for production of goods and services to increase effects of scale. Comparably populous developing nations have the chance of practical success and can encounter fewer problems regarding mobilization of a qualified workforce. Today, there are plenty of such countries in world economics. Thus, the question is what potential they have to increase the effects of scale in the production of innovational products (goods and services).

It is not easy to answer this question, as it means we will discuss the future of the world economics instead of current development. Consecutive and irreversible preparation of world society is not easy, especially not against the background of unequal and fragmented growth of ongoing changes (developed countries, especially large economies) in world economics for new paradigms and technical innovations. It ties people to achievements of technical progress but saves energy and time for their spiritual development. Deriving from the current challenges, most American scientist-economists (including Nobel Laureates in Economics R. Lucas, R. Johns, Harris, P. Krugman, M. Obstfeld, et al.), on the basis of labor distribution within world economics and the vital cycle theory of the product, presume that application of the increasing effect theory of the production scale mostly manifests results in the directions of world trade development and the composition (trade flows) thereof.

In other words, ongoing economic integration amongst developed countries will be subordinated to cooperation and specialization processes in manufacture of intellectual product organized based on the increasing effect of the scale.

The small open developed economies will occupy highly specialized niches in manufacture of the product and will cooperate with niche production along with large open economics.

Mass production of industrial capital goods (and main food products) will move to developed large open economies (for instance, Russia, India, China, Brazil, Argentina, etc.), and production of intellectual goods and services of particular category (less capital semi-prepared goods) will occur in prosperous countries possessing intellectual potential and qualified personnel.

It is crystal clear that if events and processes are developed according to this logic, then small, open, developing economies will manufacture the products and goods for foreign trade, in the production of which no increasing effect of scale is obtained. Conditions are already being developed for the initial phase of the new technologic cycle for production and service of the products of single intellectual fields (Gogorishvili, 2011). Preferences are forming for the innovational development of Georgian economy under the global crisis conditions.

The following aspects shall comply with the significant preconditions (which define the rate of the developed and developing countries in the global labor distribution system) of sustainable economic development of the world economy in the new technological cycle: developed labor resources and national educational system, as well as provision of integration (involvement) of the hereof system into the regional scientific-educational spheres.

The most important reference point for the sustainable economic development of an economy is the availability of developed labor resources. In this respect, we should distinguish two periods:

- Short run, which involves one of the phases of the long cycle of the world economic development (from the global crisis to the next crisis). The demand for labor resources is volatile according to the phases of the economic cycle in the global market. The labor resource structure is volatile as well. Therefore the competences of the international financial and economic organizations should cover recommendation-making for developing countries based on the study and forecasts of changes in labor demand. Recommendations of this kind (if fulfilled by developing countries) should bear financial responsibility for results.

Only special and secondary-special educational systems (excluding gymnasia) should address the short-term development of labor resources in developing countries. Matching higher education with the short-term-oriented structure of labor resources is costly and less effective.

- Long run, in which structural and cyclical changes usually determine the volatility of demand for labor resources and their structure. These changes are followed by both types of unemployment (structural and cyclical) which are very hard for a society, as it is never ready to face them. Not only low-skilled workers but also high-skilled ones mostly rely on trade unions, which do not exist at all in some developing countries or are absolutely inert (recent developments show that the situation is not better in developed countries either). As for the most active part of the society—politicians—unfortunately, they are focused on only short-term (election-to-election) effects. Therefore, neither the structure nor the level of qualification and development of labor resources meets the requirements of national market globalization in the long run.

The specifications and challenges of the technological cycle of the post global economic crisis period shall define the structures of economies of the developed and developing countries. Financing the volume of such changes goes beyond economic capacities of the developing countries. Consequently, the processes of sustainable development are impeded.

For developing countries to have real prospects of sustainable development, the sustainable development of the world economy should have no alternative. Only internationally coordinated efforts can solve this problem. In our view, there is a need for global management and coordination of national higher education systems within the interests of the world economy. The approved and applied practices of financing educational projects (mainly secondary education projects funded by the World Bank) do not meet the challenges of the global economy (Gogorishvili, 2014).

The delay in the Bologna Process was due to the absence of the organization which would bear the responsible for making and implementing global educational policy. Educational policy should be the essential component of the global economic policy (global order).

Among the national educational policy indicators, knowledge economy and knowledge indices are important. In developing countries, the desired value of change of these indices (during the sixth world technological cycle) will never stay only within the constraints of national efforts, because if it did, the potential opportunities of high skilled labor resource formation would be lost. Such course goes against the development interests. At present, labor resource outsourcing used by developed countries is insufficient (brings costs). At the same time, the outsourcing developing countries should follow with the goal of creation of knowledge economy and development is also ineffective. The reason behind this is the absence of efficient international policy implementation bodies. The economic use of the colossal investments made in the knowledge economy and educational systems (what can be realized only by a joint organization exerting coordination and control) will save huge amounts of financial and material resources of the world economy.

GLOBALIZATION OF MARKETS AND THE ROLE OF SMES IN ESCAPING THE "DEVELOPMENT TRAP"

This part of the essay is devoted to seeking ways to escape the problem of the "development trap." First, the "development trap" problem is studied, and second, the SMEs' special role is discussed in the escaping the "development trap." Generally, the role of education is highlighted in the research and the function of state and international organizations, as the creators of the main frame in this process is estimated. It is mentioned that due to market globalization, competition became globalized and the development trap is not only a problem for developing countries. Vulnerable groups or individuals are involved in the "trap," and the way to escape from this condition is making education more available and thus of SMEs.

The research base consists of reports from international organizations, such as the International Labor Organization, the World Bank, and the OECD, and relevant scientific publications, as well.

Considering the issue of escaping "development trap" is the little part of an old question: "Why are some countries/groups/individuals are rich and why are some are poor?" From our point of view, this is better able to explain groups and individuals' condition than whole countries'. There are many "traps" for development in our life. The meaning of this term varies depending on country and subject. Some interpretations include "welfare trap" "poverty trap," and "unemployment trap."

For example, in the United States, where government benefit payments are colloquially referred to as "welfare" (e.g., a person is "on welfare"), the welfare trap often indicates that a person is completely dependent on benefits, with little or no hope of self-sufficiency. The welfare trap is also known as the unemployment trap or poverty trap in the UK, with both terms frequently being used interchangeably as they often go hand in hand, though there are subtle differences.

In other contexts, the terms "welfare trap" and "poverty trap" are clearly distinguished. For example, a Southern African Regional Poverty Network report on social protection clarifies the poverty trap to mean a structural condition from which people cannot rescue themselves despite their best efforts. A welfare trap in this context, by contrast, refers to the barrier created by means-tested social grants that have built-in perverse incentives. This South African definition is typically used with regard to developing countries. The *unemployment trap* occurs when the net income difference between low-paid work and *unemployment benefits* is less than work-related costs, discouraging movement into work. The *poverty trap* refers to the position when *means-tested benefit* payments are reduced as income rises, combined with income tax and other deductions, with the effect of discouraging higher-paid work whether that involves working longer hours or acquiring skills (source: welfare trap, definition).

We are more likely to embrace the idea that the "development trap" is the condition of individuals when they have not the means for revealing personal skills and possibilities and are forced to work in lower-level jobs. This is close to the definition of the welfare trap. It is not always close to the poverty trap but may be one reason for it.

The "development trap" may describe countries, regions, some social groups, or individuals. It depends on different factors. The measurement of a development trap is rather difficult, and one should instead consider the poverty trap, as some statistics gives one this opportunity.

Considering the recent ILO report, it is evident that **poverty remains among the acute problems.**

In 2000, at the outset of the Millennium Development Goals, world leaders agreed to halve extreme poverty worldwide over the period 1990–2015. This target was achieved. Indeed, the rate of extreme poverty (measured from 2008 as living on less than $1.25 per day in 2005 purchasing power parity (PPP) terms) reached 10 percent in 2015, compared with 30 percent in 1990. The decline in extreme poverty was particularly pronounced in developing countries, where the rate fell from 47 percent in 1990 to 14 percent in 2015.

In the context of the 2030 Agenda for Sustainable Development, the poverty alleviation objective has been updated and carried forward. The first Sustainable Development Goal of United Nations is to "end poverty in all its forms everywhere." It includes several poverty-related targets, including ensuring appropriate social protection, equal rights to economic resources and access to basic services for all men and women (World Employment, ILO, 2016, p. 7). Despite these achievements, close to 1 billion people are living in extreme poverty globally. Moreover, if the poverty line is raised to include the moderately poor, people with income or consumption below $3.10 PPP per day, the number is more than doubled, reaching 2 billion people, or 36.2 percent of the emerging and developing world's population (World Employment, ILO, 2016, p. 9). Moreover, poverty has increased in developed countries. The at-risk-of-poverty rate in the European Union (EU) (defined as the share of the population with an income below the 60 percent of the median equivalized disposable income) remained rather stable, at around 16.5 percent, in the years leading up to the 2008 global financial crisis. Since then, this rate has trended upwards, reaching 17.2 percent of the EU population by 2014 (World Employment, ILO, 2016, p. 10). Additionally, according to the World Bank data, the GINI index rose in Estonia, Bulgaria, Greece, Hungary, Ireland, Italy, Lithuania, Luxembourg, Romania, Norway, Slovenia, Sweden (Worldbank Data— *http://data.worldbank.org/indicator/SI.POV.GINI*). Inequality in income distributions is the source of disproportional development. This means that overcoming problems with income distribution and development not only "poor" countries challenge.

The global financial-economic crisis of 2008 deepened existing gaps and created new challenges for development. Conditions of some individuals, vulnerable groups, regions, and sometimes the whole country worsened. The openness of markets and activities of transnational companies, in our opinion, helped state institutes lose all or some of their ability to overcome social problems. Globalization of markets helps increase competition and create an uncontrollable situation to escape the development trap. (It does not mean that countries must be closed.)

As labor, capital, education, and product markets are globalized, competition is globalized too. One way out of this situation is stimulation from SMEs.

There is no standard definition of what constitutes SMEs, but scientists, policymakers, researchers of international organizations almost all agree that small and medium-sized entrepreneurs play an important role in the world economy. The Edinburgh Group researchers have noted that "the contribution made by SMEs does vary widely between countries and regions. Nevertheless, although they play particularly key roles in high-income countries, SMEs are also important to low-income countries, making significant contributions to both GDP and employment. They are also major contributors in innovation economies, partly with the larger corporate sector ... When combines the data for those countries for which good data are available, SMEs account for 52% of private sector value added, which provides a reasonable estimate for the sector's global economic contribution" (Growing the Global Economy, p. 7).

Certain research outcomes suggest that rather than directly subsidizing SMEs and aiming for a large number of small enterprises, policymakers should focus on creating a business environment that allows easy entry and exit for firms and assures entrepreneurs and financiers that property rights and contracts will be enforced (Beck and Demirgüç-Kunt, 2004, p. 4). This is the right way, but we suppose that due to the abovementioned outcomes, using only this policy is not a guaranteed escape from the development trap.

CONCLUSION

Thus, we offer the following solutions:

- Formation of clusters based on the fundamental research of competitive advantages.
- Development of the entrepreneurial universities within the clusters where the links between education, science, and business will be effective.
- Formation of close relations between entrepreneurial universities with the secondary education schools. Here it is necessary to lead the professional orientation system to reveal the competitive advantage of the local economy in order to encourage pupils to develop entrepreneurial attitudes. Such an approach will foster the entrepreneurial or scientific spirit even in school-age children. It will

contribute to identifying a real competitive advantage of local economy. And as a result, as M. Porter writes: "Clusters can maintain vibrancy as competitive locations for centuries, and most successful clusters prosper at least for decades" (Porter, 2008, p. 259).

The above-mentioned international organization should have at its disposal certain directive instruments for educational and knowledge policy implementation. Such instruments comprise:

- means to overcome and temporarily eliminate obstacles revealed as a result of the world intellectual product market research:
- setting preconditions to determine the legal framework within which to produce, position in the market, and sell intellectual products;
- formation of the general frame conditions of the global legal environment for innovation design;
- design of the general framework for the global legal environment of innovations;
- design of the mechanisms for resolving conflict between the global legal environment of innovations and national systems.
- study of the activities of the economic agents operating in international markets of innovative products and elaboration of the analysis-based coordinative mechanisms;
- enhancement of competition in international markets of innovative products, with the goals to:
  1. form international rules and opportunities for setting up competition;
  2. create an international order for competition protection;
  3. develop mechanisms for the prevention of economic agents' efforts of market abuse and exert control over the outcomes of their activities;

- making short-term and long-term forecasts of innovative product market development;
- creation of the framework for international scientific and educational system, including:
    1. design of the long-term goal catalog at the mega level (the "customer" of this activity should be the international organization for educational and knowledge policy implementation);
    2. creation of the material and technical basis in accordance with the long-term goal catalog (mobilization of financial, capital and labor resources), which should ensure (this time at the meso-level) that the university and special educational institution unions be set up based on regional, branch-specific, or other principles;
    3. at the meso-level, the operation of the university and special educational institution unions, ensuring that the intermediate tasks of the goal catalogue be fulfilled and related issues settled (the parties ordering fulfillment of the intermediate tasks could be the International Organization for Global Educational and Knowledge Policy Implementation, national science and educational systems or both);
    4. at the national level, the performance of regional science and educational centers (unions) and the highest possible support for their activities as the basis for the development of higher and special educational institutions.

The goal catalog of existing international organizations is focused only on success in the world economy. At the same time, economic success can only be an intermediate task through the process of societal development. Development of a society is in causal relationships with the supreme goal of human development. Resolution of the mega-problems of human development requires huge efforts made by world intellectual resources. Now is the time to link education and knowledge orientation with human development directions on international levels.

We share the hypothesis of "culture of poverty" and think it is in high correlation with the development gap. Globalization of competition creates a complex environment, influencing the "culture of poverty." The best way is by giving individuals the opportunity to realize possibilities and get decent work. It may begin with making education more available. The state, as an institution, is responsible for providing this process and international organizations should help it. **Strategic framework for government policy** should include (according to UNESCO reports) ten steps to build skills and pathways for a better future:

1. Provide second-chance education for those with few or no basic skills. Second-chance education can provide children and youth who did not complete primary school with an opportunity to develop basic skills. Effective second-chance education requires well-coordinated and adequately funded programs at scale.
2. Tackle the barriers that limit access to lower-secondary education. Improving access to lower-secondary school means abolishing school fees and providing targeted financial support, linking lower secondary to primary schools, providing a common core curriculum so that all children are equipped with core skills, ensuring that there are enough government school places and assuring accessibility in rural areas.
3. Make upper-secondary education more accessible to the disadvantaged and improve its relevance to work. Secondary education should balance technical/vocational and general subjects and develop the capacity of students to solve problems. Flexible opportunities should be given for

youth at risk of dropping out, including distance-education centers, with greater recognition of the skills gained through such alternative learning centers.

4. Give poor urban youth access to skills training for better jobs. Public interventions that build on traditional apprenticeship systems should strengthen training by master craftspeople, improve working conditions for apprentices and ensure that skills can be certified through national qualification frameworks.

5. Aim policies and programs at youth in deprived rural areas. Farmer field schools and training through cooperatives build skills and provide training in agricultural techniques. Training in entrepreneurship and financial management widens opportunities in non-farm activities.

6. Link skills training with social protection for the poorest young people. Combining microfinance or social protection with training in basic literacy and numeracy, as well as livelihood skills, can help to tackle the multiple forms of disadvantage that keep people trapped in poverty.

7. Prioritize the training needs of disadvantaged young women. Providing young women with microfinance, livelihood assets, stipends to tide them over until these assets start to yield income, and the skills needed to make the best use of these assets gives them greater control over their resources in ways that benefit them and their families.

8. Harness the potential of technology to enhance opportunities for young people. Basic technology, such as radio, can be important in skills training, particularly for people in remote rural areas.

9. Improve planning by strengthening data collection and coordination of skills programs. Government leadership is important to coordinate the range of actors involved in skills training, reducing fragmentation and duplication of

effort and assuring equitable access. Data are needed to monitor accessibility of skills-development programs so that they can be planned effectively. This includes more information on school dropouts and completion and details on academic as well as technical and vocational areas. Better data are also needed on skills-development programs beyond the formal school system, including informal apprenticeships, linking these data with information on the labor market. Governments also need to work more closely with businesses and trade unions to improve the relevance of skills training in the workplace.
10. Mobilize additional funding dedicated to the training of disadvantaged young people.

REFERENCES

Akayev A., Hirooka M. 2009. On a mathematical model to predict the long-term dynamics of innovation—Economic Development. *Journal Reports of the Academy of Sciences, Publishing Science* (M.), Vol. 425, No. 6, pp. 727–732.

Awbrey, S. M., 2003. MAKING THE 'INVISIBLE HAND' VISIBLE: The Case for Dialogue About Academic Capitalism, *The Oakland Journal*, 2003, Spring, No. 4, pp. 33–49. http://www2.oakland.edu/oujournal/files/5_Awbrey.pdf

Beck, Thorsten & Demirgüç-Kunt, Asli, 2004. *SMEs, Growth, and Poverty*. World Bank Group, 27.

Commission Staff Working Document SEC, 2008. THE CONCEPT OF CLUSTERS AND CLUSTER POLICIES AND THEIR ROLE FOR COMPETITIVENESS AND INNOVATION: MAIN STATISTICAL RESULTS AND LESSONS LEARNED, 2637, Annex to the Communication from the Commission "Toward world-class clusters in the European Union: Implementing the broad-based innovation strategy" COM(2008)652 final of 17.10.2008, Europe Innova/PRO INNO Europe paper No. 9, pp. 24–27.

Etzkowitz, H. & Zhou, Ch., 2008. Introduction to special issue Building the entrepreneurial university: a global perspective, *Science and Public Policy*, 35(9), November 2008, p. 629; DOI: 10.3152/030234208X363178. http://www.ingentaconnect.com/content/beech/spp

Fostering Small and Medium Sized Enterprises (SMEs)' Participation in Global Markets, 2012. *OECD Secretariat,* February 2012.

Fredua-Kwarteng, E., 2005. Enhancing Secondary Education in Ghana: The case of Entrepreneurship. OISE/ University of Toronto. ED493192. Education Resources Information Center (http://eric.ed.gov); [online] www.files.eric.ed.gov/fulltext/ED493192.pdf

Gagnidze, I. and Maisuradze, N., 2016. "Systemic effects of international educational and scientific links. Proposals for the development of educational and scientific national system in Georgia," *Int. J. Markets and Business Systems*, forthcoming in Vol. 2, No. 1, pp. 25–44.

Gogorishvili, I., 2011. Formation of preferences of the innovational development of Georgian economics under the global crisis conditions. The 3rd International Conference "Globalization and Prospects of Economic Development of Georgia," Tbilisi State University, December 2011, Tbilisi, pp. 20–25.

Gogorishvili, I., 2014. Sustainable economic development and global crisis.Business Systems Laboratory 2ND International Symposium. Systems Thinking for a Sustainable Economy. Advancements in Economic and Managerial Theory and Practice. January 23–24, 2014. Universitas Mercatorum. Rome, http://bslab-symposium.net/

Growing the Global Economy through SMEs, Edinburg Group http://www.edinburgh-group.org/media/2776/edinburgh_group_ research_-_growing_the_global_economy_through_smes.pdf

Guerrero, M. & Urbano, D. The Development of an entrepreneurial university, J Technol Transf DOI 10.1007/s10961-010-9171-x Springer Science+Business Media, LLC 2010, p. 5.

Hatak, I. & Reiner, E., 2011. *Entrepreneurship Education in Secondary Schools: Education systems, teaching methods and best practice—a survey of Austria, Finland, France, Germany, Italy, Spain, Sweden, Vienna, Austria.*

Hirooka, M., 2006. Innovation Dynamism and Economic Growth. A Nonlinear Perspective. Cheltenham, UK; Northampton, MA, USA. "Edward Elgar," pp. 426.

Ketels, Ch., 2015. *Competitiveness and Clusters: Implications for a New European Growth Strategy*, Working Paper no. 84, Welfare, Wealth, Work for Europe, pp. 25–28.

Kondratieff, N., 1935. The Long Waves in Economic Life. *Review of Economics and Statistics,* Vol. 18, no. 6, pp. 105–115.

Korotaev, A. & Tsirel, S., 2010. A Spectral Analysis of World GDP Dynamics: Kondratieff Waves, Kuznets Swings, Juglar and Kitchin Cycles in Global Economic Development, and the 2008–2009 Economic Crisis. Structure and Dynamics, Vol. 4, No. 1, pp. 1–55. Available online:http://www.escholarship.org/uc/item/9jv108xp [accessed April 14, 2011].

Kyrö, P. & Mattila, J., 2012. Toward future university by integrating Entrepreneurial and the 3rd Generation University concepts, pp. 4–5. *See in:* Wissema,, J. G. (2009). *Toward the Third Generation University: Managing the University in Transition.* Edward Elgar.

Mayer-Foulkes, D., 2006. *Globalization and the Human Development Trap,* CIDE, Mexico, December 28th, 2006.

Mensch, G., 2006. If this Long Wave Steeps-Up and Breaks: What then? Kondratieff Waves.Warfare and World Security.—T. C. Deveras (Ed.)—IOS Press, p. 80–90.

Mensh, G., 1979. Stalemate in Technology—Innovation Overcame the Depression. New York: Ballinger Publishing Company.

NOTICES FROM EUROPEAN UNION INSTITUTIONS AND BODIES COUNCIL, 2009. Conclusions of the Council and of the Representatives of the Governments of the Member States, meeting within the Council, of 26 November 2009 on developing the role of education in a fully- functioning knowledge triangle, (2009/C 302/03), p. 3. [online] http://eur-lex.europa.eu/legal-content/EN/TXT/PDF/?uri=OJ:C:2009:302:FULL&from=EN

OECD, 2008. *Enhancing the Role of SMEs in Global Value Chains.*

Porter, M. E., 1998. *The Competitive Advantage of Nations,* With a new Introduction, Manufactured in the United States of America. THE FREE PRESS. ISBN 0-684-84147-9.

Porter, M. E., 2008. *On Competition.* Updated and Expanded Edition, The Harvard business review book series, ISBN 978-1-4221-2696-7.

THE ROLE OF SMES AND ENTREPRENEURSHIP IN A GLOBALIZED ECONOMY, 2009. EXPERT REPORT NUMBER 34 TO SWEDEN'S GLOBALISATION COUNCIL, THE GLOBALISATION COUNCIL 2009

Shumpeter, J. A., 1934. The Theory of Economic Development. Cambridge, Mass., 1934, Ch. II.

Shumpeter, J. A., 1939. *Business Cycles: A Theoretical, Historical and Statistical Analysis of Capitalist Processes.* New York: Macmillan. Vol. I.

UNESCO, 2012. *Education for All Global Monitoring Report.*

UNESCO, 2015. *EDUCATION FOR ALL 2000–2015: achievements and challenges,*

Vestergaard, L., 2015. *Entrepreneurship in Education in the Baltic Sea Region, A report under EUSBSR Priority Area 8: Implementing the Small Business Act, Danish Foundation for Entrepreneurship—Young Enterprise.* February. ISBN: 978-87-90386-10-8, Denmark.

Welfare_trap, definition, https://en.wikipedia.org/wiki/Welfare_trap

World Economic Forum, 2015. The Inclusive Growth and Development Report 2015

World Employment and Social Outlook 2016: Transforming jobs to end poverty, International Labor Office—Geneva: ILO, 2016.

Worldbank Data. http://data.worldbank.org/indicator/SI.POV.GINI

CONCLUSIONS
SMES AND NEW SUSTAINABLE LEADERS 2018

Eva Kras

This book involves youth 20 years hence (or sooner) and work possibilities—which at present does not look as very viable, as we continue to place (as a society) "money first and humanity second." This will change as societies begin to see youth with imagination and the development of strong communities, so youth do not feel lonely and lost in their search for work.

From the standpoint of the many aspects of present-day youth, certain qualities appear to be the most pertinent:

1.) Getting used to large companies (and others) constantly saying "no jobs," and how this affects youth even now, as they struggle to find work. We hear little reaction from parents, except "lack of understanding" is sometimes mentioned, as parents feel "they have given so much money" to their offspring to keep them happy and well educated.

2.) Now we have a new situation where some youth are working at various jobs to make money, as they see money as the key to getting ahead in our present world. Others just give up, feel depressed, and often turn to harmful activities, as they have been turned down so many times with nothing on the horizon.

3.) We must create a newer situation for youth (present or 20 years hence). First, we need to use the "imagination of youth." This is where SMEs come into play, together with strong local communities. If a young person sees some "light at the end of the tunnel," that is wonderful.

This means hard work from the individual.

a.) Youth need to study (or learn from other SMEs) how this works, and especially the importance of strong communities, so youth have someone to talk to, and go from feeling "alone" to "belonging" in place.

b.) Youth must begin to realize that society around them will not emphasize "money" but are changing to the importance of "humanity." This is huge. The new world will be emphasizing SMEs and accepting incomes which are still decent, as it involves a house or place to live, health and education for offspring, and friends and neighbors with similar ways of thinking. This places society in general on a different plane. Others value us for our human values, and not for our "money" as in the past.

To summarize, this involves:

a.) Going from large international companies to SMEs.
b.) The importance of "solid communities" to which we all belong.

c.) "Sharing" with others, in place of "competition" constantly.
d.) Thinking about this from an early age—even in elementary school.
e.) Education for new and applicable learning in business schools—a huge job for post-secondary education, and universities.
f.) Governments and huge changes and new needs for SMEs.
g.) Trade becoming local trade within a nation or its very near neighbors—all SMEs (There will still be a few large companies, but they will be different).

Welcome to the new world of change!
It changes how we think every day.
WELCOME!

ACKNOWLEDGMENTS

Firstly, I would like to recognize and thank my publisher, John Koehler. Without his understanding of the subject at hand and his incredible personal aspects (the human touch) this book would not have been possible.

Regarding the many living examples of what is possible, we want to recognize all who wrote papers for this book. You are the core of this book, and we thank you deeply for your contributions.

We would like to recognize Carolin Rekar, Rosalinda Sanquiche, and Jacques Chiriazi especially for their contributions.

We also want to recognize the efforts of all the people who contributed time and effort in the marketing of this book in Europe, North America, and Latin America.

We especially want to recognize the principal directors for three regions of the world: Nicolas Grepe (for North and Latin America) and Vasja Roblek (for Europe).

There are too many other people involved in this concept to mention everyone, but we thank you all for your contributions.

WE LIVE IN INTERESTING, CHANGING TIMES!

ABOUT THE CONTRIBUTORS

Peter Soderbaum
Peter Soderbaum is a professor emeritus in ecological economics at Mälardalen University in Västerås, Sweden. He advocates a more human and politically conscious view of the world.

Carolin Rekar Munro
As a leadership consultant managing Eye of the Tiger Consulting, Carolin collaborates with leaders on change management, employee engagement, strategic planning, performance management, and developing teams. Carolin is also professor in the leadership MBA program at Royal Roads University in Victoria, British Columbia. She is also adjunct professor in the master's education program at Central Michigan University and a visiting professor at Mount Meru University in Tanzania. She is co-owner of Monarch Safari Guides, based in Tanzania.

Darcy Hitchcock
Darcy has a knack for translating the theory of sustainability into practical and actionable tools. She is the author of the award-winning

book, *The Business Guide to Sustainability*, as well as *Great Work: 12 Principles for Your Work Life and Life's Work*. She spent over fifteen years as a sustainability consultant and cofounded the International Society of Sustainability Professionals and the Sustainability Alliance of Northern Arizona.

Jacques Chirazi
Jacques is a specialist in many aspects of ecology, including biomimicry, project management, strategy consulting, financial analysis, marketing, market research, and mergers and acquisitions analysis. He also has expertise in climate change, mitigation and adoption policies, renewable energy, waste to energy, smart cities technologies, and international environmental treaties. He is a certified energy manager. He speaks, reads, and writes fluently in French and English and is conversant in Spanish and German. At present, Jacques works in California.

Maria Teresa Bianchi
Maria Teresa is an assistant professor of business administration at Sapienza University of Rome in Italy. She serves as a member of an editorial board reviewing several academic journals, is an associate fellow at the EuroMed Research Business Institute, is a member of the Italian Association of Professors in Accounting and Business Administration (SIDREA), and is the author of several scientific books and articles. Her research interests include corporate governance, financial accounting, corporate social responsibility, turnarounds, and integrated welfare.

Ineza Gagnidze
Ineza is working as an associate professor of economics and business at Tbilisi State University in Georgia. She belongs to a number of associations, such as European Studies for Innovative Development in Georgia, and has also taken part in several international projects, such as those at Brunel University, the Piraeus Technological Education

Institute and Piraeus University in Greece, and the University of Paris 8 in France. Ineza is a member of the scientific board of Business Systems Laboratories as well as an editorial member of the *International Journal of Markets and Business Systems* and a member of the advisory board of Cambridge Scholars Publishing. Her main research interests are education, sustainable development, clusters, and systems thinking.

Irina Gogorishvili

Irina is an associate professor of economics and business at Tbilisi State University in Georgia and a member of the Georgian-German Institute for Economic Policy and Economic Education. She participated in the Winter School of 96 with the Lifelong Learning Institute and several projects for the University of Paris 8 and Bremen University. She is a member of five scientific boards for Business Systems Laboratories as well as the scientific board of the international journal *Estonian Discussions on Economic Policy*. Her main research areas are economic policy, international economy, social entrepreneurship, and educational systems.

Nino Papachashvili

Nino holds a PhD of Economics and is currently Associate Professor at the Faculty of Economics and Business at Ivane Javakhishvili Tbilisi State University (Georgia) where she teaches International Economics. She participated in a number of grant projects funded by HESP, ASCN, and the Estonian Development Cooperation, and in LLL programs. Her main fields of research focus on issues of international trade and country's integration into the world economy. She is a member of the Scientific Board of the Business Systems Laboratory (BS-Lab) association. She is the author of more than fifty scientific works and she has been editor and reviewer of more than thirty books and proceedings in the field of Economics and Business.

CPSIA information can be obtained
at www.ICGtesting.com
Printed in the USA
LVHW030022011118
595511LV00001B/23/P

9 781633 936966